Comments on other *Amazing Stories* from readers & reviewers

"You might call them the non-fiction response to Harlequin romances: easy to consume and potentially addictive."

Robert Martin, *The Chronicle Herald*

"Tightly written volumes filled with lots of wit and humour about famous and infamous Canadians."

Eric Shackleton, *The Globe and Mail*

"This is popular history as it should be... For this price, buy two and give one to a friend."

Terry Cook, a reader from Ottawa, on **Rebel Women**

"Stories are rich in description, and bristle with a clever, stylish realness."

Mark Weber, *Central Alberta Advisor*, on **Ghost Town Stories II**

"The resulting book is one readers will want to share with all the women in their lives."

Lynn Martel, *Rocky Mountain Outlook*, on **Women Explorers**

"[The books are] long on plot and character and short on the sort of technical analysis that can be dreary for all but the most committed academic."

Robert Martin, *The Chronicle Herald*

"A compelling read. Bertin ... has selected only the most intriguing tales, which she narrates with a wealth of detail."

Joyce Glasner, *New Brunswick Reader*, on **Strange Events**

"The heightened sense of drama and intrigue, good dose of human interest, is what sets Amaz

Pamela Klaffke, *Calgary Heral*

TECUMSEH

AMAZING STORIES®

TECUMSEH

Diplomat and Warrior
in the War of 1812

Irene Ternier Gordon

BIOGRAPHY

James Lorimer & Company Ltd., Publishers
Toronto

James Lorimer & Company Ltd., Publishers acknowledge the support of the Ontario Arts Council. We acknowledge the support of the Government of Canada through the Book Publishing Industry Development Program (BPIDP) for our publishing activities. We acknowledge the support of the Canada Council for the Arts for our publishing program. We acknowledge the support of the Government of Ontario through the Ontario Media Development Corporation's Ontario Book Initiative.

ONTARIO ARTS COUNCIL
CONSEIL DES ARTS DE L'ONTARIO

Canada Council
for the Arts

Library and Archives Canada Cataloguing in Publication

Gordon, Irene Ternier
Tecumseh : diplomat and warrior in the War of 1812 / Irene Ternier Gordon.

(Amazing stories)
Includes bibliographical references.
ISBN 978-1-55277-430-4

1. Tecumseh, Shawnee Chief, 1768-1813. 2. Indians of North America—Wars—1812-1815. 3. Shawnee Indians—Kings and rulers—Biography. 4. Tenskwatawa, Shawnee Prophet, 1775?-1834. 5. Shawnee Indians—Biography. I. Title. II. Series: Amazing stories (Toronto, Ont.)

E99.S35T147 2009   974.004'973170092   C2009-904001-8

James Lorimer & Company Ltd., Publishers
317 Adelaide Street West, Suite 1002
Toronto, Ontario
M5V 1P9
www.lorimer.ca

Printed and bound in Canada

Mixed Sources
Cert no. SW-COC-001271
© 1996 FSC
FSC

To my son-in-law Travis Dudych. It has long been his ambition to have a book dedicated to him. This is especially for you, Travis.

Acknowledgements

Thank you to Ron Dale, an expert on the War of 1812, who offered me much valuable assistance during the editing of my book. The lines of verse introducing each chapter are taken from *Tecumseh: A Drama*, by Charles Mair, 1886.

Contents

Introductory Note

It is virtually impossible to determine the accuracy of much of the available information about Tecumseh, especially about his early life, because he left no written records. During his lifetime — from about 1768 to 1813 — few Shawnee could read or write. The few contemporary accounts that exist were written by people whom likely had never met Tecumseh or had little first-hand knowledge of him. Often these writers were hostile towards the Shawnee.

Prologue

Tecumseh opened his eyes and stretched his cramped muscles as he woke from an uneasy sleep. He was lying in the tangled mass of uprooted trees and broken branches left by a recent tornado. The motionless air was hot and heavy with moisture, and insects buzzed annoyingly about his head. Dense, leaden-grey clouds hung close to the ground like fog. Although it was barely daylight, he suspected it was several hours past sunrise.

Adding to his discomfort was hunger. Warriors were used to fasting and lying in wait before a battle, but this was his third day without food. Many of the other warriors had gone looking for food the previous day, but Tecumseh had promised that none of the small advance party he was leading would leave their post before the enemy appeared. Surely the enemy would come today. If they didn't, Tecumseh realized that his men would have to break cover to find food before nightfall.

Within a few minutes, a thunderstorm blew up. Scouts brought word that it was unlikely that the enemy would march that day, so many of the remaining warriors sought food and shelter in the camp that had grown up around the nearby British post of Fort Miami. Tecumseh was tempted to follow them, but he decided to wait until noon in case the storm blew over quickly. It was a good decision. One hundred and fifty mounted American militiamen came into view about mid-morning. The long wait was over. The Battle of Fallen Timbers was about to begin.

Chapter One
The Making of a Warrior

And you remember, too, that boyish morn,
... when you and I half-dreaming lay
In summer grass, but woke to deadly pain
Of loud-blown bugles ringing through the air.
Of frontier troopers eager for the fight.

Tecumseh's Childhood

Tecumseh's first direct experience with the hated Long Knives
— the name given by the Shawnee to American militiamen
— occurred when he was aged about twelve and was old
enough to play a small part in battle. Tradition has it that he
ran to hide at the first sound of enemy fire but that no enemy
ever saw his back again between that day and his death,
some thirty years later.

It was August 1780, and America was in the midst of
the Revolutionary War. British regulars, supported by loyalist
militia and warriors, were attacking settlements in Virginia
and Kentucky. They launched their attacks from an area
near Tecumseh's birthplace — the village of Piqua on the

Mad River near present-day Springfield, Ohio. In retaliation a thousand Kentucky militiamen attacked Piqua.

Piqua was an ideal location for a town. According to an 1880 description, "The hill, the wall of rocks, the open plain carpeted with wild flowers of all colors, the silver line of the river … the long line of … wigwams [and] here and there a cornfield indicated that the Indians had selected this place not only for its natural strength, but as well for its fertility and beauty." Warriors could keep watch for enemies from the top of the nearby hill, from where they could see as far as eight kilometres up and down the river. The town itself was concealed by a heavy growth of trees, and its approach was also defended by a stockade, which was uncommon for a Native village. At one time Piqua may have had a population of nearly four thousand.

The Long Knives faced some three hundred warriors, led by Chief Catahecassa or Black Hoof. They drove the warriors from the limestone cliffs overlooking the river and then mounted their cannons on the cliffs and bombarded the stockade. By nightfall the warriors had been routed and began an orderly retreat, taking with them their women and children, who had been hidden safely outside the village before the battle began. The Americans did not pursue them, but they did burn Piqua and two neighbouring villages and destroyed more than three hundred hectares of corn. Although the loss of life was relatively small, the Shawnee were left without shelter or food.

Tecumseh's father, Chief Puckshinwah, had been killed at the Battle of Point Pleasant between the Shawnee and the Virginia militia in October 1774. As a result of this battle, the Shawnee had given up their claim to land south of the Ohio River. According to one story, albeit of doubtful historical authenticity, six-year-old Tecumseh remembered for the rest of his life what his mother Methotaske and his older brother Cheesuaka and sister Tecumapease had told him at the time. As Puckshinwah lay dying, he told Cheesuaka that he had two commands for him. First, he must never make peace with the Long Knives. Second, he must train his small brother Tecumseh to be a fierce warrior.

Methotaske explained death to Tecumseh — whose name is generally translated as "Panther Springing across the Sky" — by reminding him of the deer he had seen bounding through the forest that day. The deer was strong and beautiful until a hunter pierced his heart with an arrow. Then the deer became stiff and cold and his beauty departed. Such had happened to his father, she explained. She told Tecumseh that he must avenge the death of his father when he grew to be a man. She said that his feet would become as swift as forked lightning, his arms as strong as thunderbolts and his spirit as fearless as the cataracts that fell from mountain peaks.

Shortly after Puckshinwah's death Methotaske gave

birth to triplets. Only one, a boy named Lalawethika, lived to adulthood. Within a few years Methotaske moved south to live with relatives, leaving her younger children behind to be raised by Cheesuaka and Tecumapease.

Many events throughout Tecumseh's childhood strengthened his feelings against the American Long Knives. Chief Cornstalk, Shawnee leader at the Battle of Point Pleasant, was murdered by American militiamen in 1777. Tecumseh also remembered what his mother and Tecumapease had told him about Nonhemlina, the older sister of Cornstalk. She was a very powerful leader with her own village. Although she tried to make peace between the Shawnee and the Long Knives, she could also be a fierce warrior. Shawnee women were sometimes asked to lead warriors into battle because of a vision they had. It is said that the women did not wear any clothing in battle, and their enemies were so disconcerted by the sight of a bunch of naked women that they would run away without fighting. This story may have arisen independently among the Shawnee, however, it is so similar to ancient Celtic stories that it may have also been adopted from the Celts.

The village elders told Tecumseh and the other children the story of their tribe. They said that the grandmother and grandfather of the Shawnee came out of the great salt water, where the sun rose each morning. The land where they had lived before had been swallowed up in the great salt water by

Charge of the Dragoons at Fallen Timbers, by R. T. Zogbaum

an evil spirit. Everyone in the land died except for the grandmother and the grandfather, who were saved by good spirits.
The grandmother was brought safely to shore holding onto
the tail of a panther and the grandfather was carried to the
shore by a huge swan. These two became the first people of
the Shawnee (meaning "Water People") tribe, whose totems
are the panther and the swan.

When Tecumseh was about ten years old three frontiersmen stole some horses from the Shawnee town of Chillicothe.
They would have got away if they had been content with

taking one or two horses each, but they stole a whole herd. This slowed their movements so much that the furious owners caught up with them. One of the men escaped, the second was killed, and the third — a man named Simon Kenton — was captured and dragged back to Chillicothe. At Chillicothe, Kenton was confronted by Chief Blackfish, who roared out in excellent English, "You have been stealing horses?" When Kenton admitted that he had, Blackfish whipped him across his bare back and shoulders with a hickory switch and marched him into the village.

Tecumseh was visiting Chillicothe on the day that Kenton was taken prisoner. Tecumseh, along with everyone else in the village, ran out to see the prisoner. They yelled abuse at him as Kenton was stripped naked and tied to a stake with his hands raised over his head. The villagers danced around the stake until midnight, screaming at Kenton, whipping and slapping him. The next day he was forced to run the gauntlet — two rows of people armed with weapons, with which they struck him as he ran between them. Then a council was held to decide if Kenton should be burned at the stake immediately or if he should first be exhibited in the neighbouring villages. After the warriors completed their deliberations, Blackfish handed a large war club to the circle of men. Those in favour of immediate burning struck the club violently on the ground before passing it on to the next man. Those opposed passed the club on silently. The council was opposed to killing Kenton immediately. Although Tecumseh hated the Long Knives and was angry that they had tried to steal Shawnee horses, he was disturbed by the torture of Kenton. He promised himself that he would not torture anyone when he became a warrior.

As an adult, Tecumseh would have several encounters with Simon Kenton, who finally escaped after spending many months as a prisoner of the Shawnee and later of the British. In 1792, the Shawnee set up camp on the Kentucky frontier as a base from which to steal horses from the settlers. Kenton and some followers snuck up to the camp one night, hoping to frighten the Shawnee into abandoning it. However, Tecumseh leapt from his tent and led an attack that drove Kenton and his men away. The following year Kenton and Tecumseh met again when Kenton led a dawn attack on a Shawnee hunting camp. The plan failed when one of the frontiersmen fired prematurely and the Shawnee disappeared. While the frontiersmen plundered the empty camp, Tecumseh rounded up their horses. Then the Shawnee rode off, leaving the Kentuckians to walk home.

Tecumseh met Simon Kenton again in 1802. This time they talked to each other instead of fighting. In 1799 Kenton and six other families from Kentucky had moved to Ohio and founded the town of Springfield. But three years later Kenton had decided that he needed more land, so he asked Tecumseh to sell him the Shawnee lands between the Miami and Wabash rivers. Tecumseh accepted a generous payment for the land, knowing full well that the Shawnee had already signed it away by a treaty with the Americans. Tecumseh, who refused to sign any treaties, was delighted to put one over on his old enemy.

Tecumseh's childhood was not all death and adversity. He had many good times playing with the other boys. They ran races and jumped streams. They swam in the Mad River, they wrestled and they shot at targets with bows and arrows. All these activities were fun, but they also prepared the boys to become skillful hunters and warriors.

An entertaining story is told about Tecumseh's youth. It describes a competition between Tecumseh and some friends to see who was the best deer hunter. Early one morning, after agreeing that they would return home at sunset on the third day, each boy set off into the woods in a different direction. On the third day one boy arrived back with the skins of ten deer that he had killed. Several other boys arrived over the next few minutes. They also had ten skins each. When only a sliver of sun remained above the horizon, another boy appeared with twelve skins. Now only Tecumseh had not yet returned. The other boys joked that he must have got lost. Then, just as the sun was about to disappear completely, Tecumseh walked out of the woods. He had thirty-three skins. Unfortunately this story is of questionable accuracy.

The Child Becomes a Warrior

Tecumseh likely took part in his first real battle when he was about fifteen years old. The Shawnee attacked a fleet of flatboats on the Ohio River, killing all but one of the boatmen. The survivor was later burned at the stake. Tecumseh, according to one writer, spoke passionately against this action:

> *What bravery, what courage, what strength*
> *is there in the torturing of a man unable to*
> *defend himself? ... An enemy he was, yes!*
> *Death he deserved, yes! But the death of*
> *a man, not that of a rat cornered and tied*
> *and burned alive. How have we the right to*
> *call ourselves warriors, or even men, if we*
> *act in such a manner? ... Never again will I*
> *take part in the torture like this of any living*
> *creature, man or animal.*

One aspect of Tecumseh's character — a lifelong hatred of torture — emerges in this speech. His words and actions throughout his entire life support these views, but it is most unlikely that he would have dared to speak out so strongly as a very young man at his first battle. It is equally unlikely that there would have been anyone present to translate his words into English and to write them down. The writer does not indicate the source of this speech.

The Shawnee were divided into four groups. Tecumseh's family were members of the Kispoko branch, and his older brother Cheesuaka became war chief of the Kispoko in the 1780s. Shortly afterwards Cheesuaka and his small band travelled south to join the Chickamauga, a mixed group of warriors headed by Cherokee chief Dragging Canoe. The Shawnee and the Chickamauga fought together in several skirmishes against the Americans. Their final confrontation was the Battle of Buchanan's Station, fought near Nashville, Tennessee, on September 30, 1792.

The Chickamauga attacked about midnight. Unfortunately for them, it was a cloudless night with a full moon. The warriors repeatedly stormed the station in an effort to break down the gate, but they could easily be seen in the moonlight and the sharpshooters inside inflicted serious losses on them. The battle raged for an hour before the Chickamauga retreated in confusion with most of their leaders killed or wounded. One of the first shots in the battle killed Cheesuaka. Tecumseh, who now led the Kispoko Shawnee, returned home with his warriors. He was more determined than ever to continue fighting the Long Knives.

The Battle of Fallen Timbers
Tecumseh's first real test as a military commander came at the Battle of Fallen Timbers in August 1794. This battle was the final engagement of the Northwest Indian War

that had begun in 1785 between the Americans and a confederacy of warriors representing some dozen Native nations. The confederacy — led by Little Turtle of the Miami, Blue Jacket of the Shawnee and Roundhead of the Wyandot — agreed that they would speak with one voice in negotiations with the United States for control of the land known as the Northwest Territory. The territory stretched around the west and south shores of the Great Lakes and included the modern states of Ohio, Indiana, Illinois, Michigan, Wisconsin, and part of Minnesota.

The confederacy was unsuccessful, however. One reason for its failure was the nature of Native society, in which the rights of individuals were held sacred. Decisions were commonly made through influence or persuasion rather than enforced by a central authority. The decision to go into battle, for instance, was often made on a village or even an individual basis.

The American military leader, General "Mad Anthony" Wayne, made a final attempt to negotiate peace with the confederacy leaders in the summer of 1794. When Little Turtle suggested that they consider Wayne's peace offer, Blue Jacket and Tecumseh questioned his courage. As a result Little Turtle resigned. Blue Jacket then led the confederacy into battle, with Tecumseh as one of his top lieutenants.

More than a thousand warriors took up a defensive stand in mid-August on the rocky bank of the Maumee River (also known historically as the Miami River), which flows between Fort Wayne, Indiana, and Toledo, Ohio. The area became known as Fallen Timbers because the dense forest along the river had been hit by a tornado earlier that summer, leaving a wild tangle of uprooted trees and broken branches nearly two kilometres long.

Wayne knew that Shawnee warriors normally fasted the day before battle, so he let it be known that he intended to attack on August 17 — but then did nothing for another three days. By that time, at least five hundred of the warriors waiting in ambush had left to look for food. Those who remained were weakened by hunger. When August 20 dawned with heavy wind and rain, scouts brought word to Blue Jacket that the Americans were unlikely to move that day. As a result most of the remaining warriors went to look for food. While they were gone a thunderstorm blew up. As a result, many sought shelter in a nearby camp rather than returning to the ambush. Only about four hundred warriors remained at their posts.

Despite the weather, Wayne's army of more than 3,500 men — led by a hundred and fifty mounted Kentucky volunteer militiamen — began its final advance at about 8 a.m. As they approached Fallen Timbers they were ambushed by some 1,100 warriors and a handful of British volunteers, who had taken cover behind the tangle of trees. The militiamen turned and fled towards the main army, pursued by three or four hundred warriors. Wayne soon rallied his forces, however, and the Kentucky dragoons began to roust Blue Jacket's warriors from cover and drive them back. The initial dragoon charge faltered when their leader was killed, but the next-in-command quickly regained control. Men and horses charged over fallen trees like jockeys in a steeplechase and forced the warriors several kilometres downstream. The dragoons cut down and killed warriors with their sabres as they went. Then Wayne halted, regrouped his men and ordered them to remain on the defensive for several hours to see if Blue Jacket would mount a counterattack. They made camp when no such attack developed.

Tecumseh and his men covered Blue Jacket's retreat until Tecumseh realized that they were in danger of being surrounded by the Americans. Then, in a desperate attempt to escape, they broke cover and attacked an artillery squad that included a cannon mounted on a wagon. They cut the horses free from the wagon and rode away on them, leaving the cannon stranded. Tecumseh and his men were the last to leave the field in a battle that was over in less than an hour. Tecumseh and Blue Jacket returned to Fort Miami, where they expected that the commander, Major William Campbell, would offer them sanctuary. Unknown to the Native leaders, the British and Americans were about to sign a treaty by which the British would withdraw their garrisons from American territory. Neither side wanted war, thus Major

Campbell felt that he had to abandon the Native confederacy in order to keep the peace. Tecumseh was so angry at what he saw as Campbell's betrayal that, following the battle, he refused to meet with or accept aid from the British. While warriors from the other Nations who had fought at Fallen Timbers returned to their homes, the Shawnee had no homes to return to because the Americans had destroyed all their villages and laid waste their fields. Many Shawnee spent the following winter in a refugee camp.

The British immediately built a large storehouse near the Shawnee camp and filled it with supplies. Twice a week clerks from the British Indian Department distributed barrels of salt pork and beef, flour, beans or peas, corn and a small amount of fresh beef. Although the Shawnee were angry at the British, they had to accept handouts from them in order to survive the winter.

The following summer the chiefs of the twelve allied tribes of the Native confederacy signed the Treaty of Greenville to officially end the Northwest Indian War. Members of the confederacy felt that their defeat at the hands of the Americans gave them no choice but to accept the loss of much of their land by the treaty. Black Hoof and Blue Jacket signed for the Shawnee. As Blue Jacket told his son, most of the tribes went to a big council at Greenville, where they made a treaty with Wayne to give much land to the Americans and they buried a hatchet.

Chapter Two
A Second Native Confederacy

And one in heart the scattered nations stood,
And one in hand. It comes! And mine shall be
The lofty task to teach them to be free —
To knit the nations, bind them into one,
And end the task great Pontiac begun!

Life after Greenville

Tecumseh, still furious at both the Americans and British, boycotted the ceremonies surrounding the signing of the Treaty of Greenville. He said that the land was on loan from the Great Spirit and thus not to be sold. Many Shawnee viewed Tecumseh as a troublemaker who usurped tribal authority. As a result, he was left with only a small group of followers.

Life was difficult for Tecumseh and his followers in the decade after the Battle of Fallen Timbers. They were often hungry because game and fur-bearing animals were in short supply, they did not have a permanent home, and they were estranged from those who had signed the Treaty of Greenville. Despite these difficulties, Tecumseh still firmly believed that all Native peoples should stand together so that they would not lose all their land to the Americans.

Potawatomi chief Simon Pokagon described how Tecumseh began organizing his confederacy. Chief Simon's account, written in 1899, was based on the eyewitness account of his father, Leopold Pokagon, who was chief between 1800 and 1840. Chief Leopold said that Tecumseh sent out runners to announce to each tribe the time when he would meet them at their council fire. Then he and two other gaily dressed chiefs travelled to each tribe, riding spirited black ponies. Tecumseh's bearing was so noble that enthusiastic cheers broke out before he even opened his mouth to speak. In a typical speech he would remind his listeners that the Great Spirit had given the land to them. He would tell them that the incoming Americans were trying to destroy the Native people and take all the land for themselves. He would accuse the settlers of being "cunning, crafty and cruel, without honour, without natural affection." He would conclude by saying that the only remedy was for all the tribes to join together and reminding them that whatever peace they had enjoyed over the past fifty years was owed entirely "to the brave Pontiac."

In 1803 a settler living near Chillicothe, Ohio, was murdered and scalped. No one ever learned who had committed the crime, but a well-respected Shawnee elder was murdered in retaliation. The elder killed one of his attackers and seriously wounded two others while trying to defend himself. Both settlers and the Shawnee were now very worried that serious hostilities would break out. Several prominent citizens of Chillicothe met with Tecumseh and his followers. Chillicothe, somewhat confusingly, was the name of at least five different Shawnee towns over the years, as well as of settler communities in several states. Because the main chief of the Shawnee could come from only the Chillicothe clan, his home town was always called Chillicothe. If the next chief came from a different town, the name switched to that community.

Tecumseh, despite his anti-American feelings, didn't want war. He vowed that the Shawnee had no connection with the murder and agreed to speak to the people of Chillicothe. One of the listeners described Tecumseh's speech. He said that Tecumseh "appeared one of the most dignified men I ever beheld" and that the vast crowd "preserved the most profound silence" while he was speaking. Tecumseh spoke so confidently of the intention of the Indians to adhere to the Treaty of Greenville and to live in peace and friendship with their white brethren that he "dispelled, as if by magic, the apprehensions of the whites."

The Making of a Prophet
Tecumseh's brother, Lalawethika, the sole survivor of the

triplets born after the death of their father in 1774, was considered a ne'er-do-well until he was in his thirties. Then he became a medicine man and co-leader of the second Native

Tens-Kwau-Ta-Waw, The Prophet, 1837

confederacy with Tecumseh.

Lalawethika had lost the sight of his right eye in a child-hood accident with an arrow, which may explain why he did not excel as either a hunter or warrior. He was often drunk, and he had trouble supporting his wife and children. Then one day he met Changing Feathers, an elderly and highly respected medicine man. Although Changing Feathers was not impressed when he first met Lalawethika, the two men gradually became friends. Finally, Changing Feathers agreed to take Lalawethika as his student. After Changing Feathers died in 1804, Lalawethika aspired to replace him as the tribe's medicine man. Gaining the respect and trust of his fellow tribesman would be difficult, however, because many still believed him to be a boastful good-for-nothing who drank too much.

In the winter of 1805, an epidemic — likely influenza — broke out among the Shawnee. Lalawethika treated the sick with herbs and prayers, but many people died. The people murmured among themselves. Many believed that Changing Feathers would have been able to cure those who had died and decided that Lalawethika could not be a true medicine man.

Lalawethika felt discouraged. One evening in early April, he was sitting by his fire pondering his future. He reached into the fire and picked up a brand to light his pipe. As he did so, he suddenly fell over, as if dead. His wife rushed out of their tent to call for help. By the time she returned, Lalawethika did not appear to be breathing. His wife carefully covered his body, and a neighbour went to tell the remainder of the village that Lalawethika was dead. Shawnee custom decreed that a body remain at home for half a day after death before it was prepared for burial by blood relatives. Just as the relatives were about to begin preparations, however, Lalawethika began to stir.

Slowly he regained his senses. He told his shocked family not to be alarmed and ordered them to call everyone together because he had an important story to tell them. His listeners sat spellbound as he described going on a journey to the spirit world, where he met the "Master of Life." He was guided on his journey by two handsome young men.

As they travelled, they came to a fork in the road. His companions told him that the right fork led to happiness and the left to misery. To the right was a place abounding in game, fish and fine cornfields, where the spirits of virtuous Shawnee could lead the same kind of life as they had on earth. The souls of sinful Shawnee, however, were forced to go to the left and enter lodges where they were punished according to the sins they had committed. For example, drunkards were offered cups of liquor resembling melted lead. Drinking this liquor brought on an agonizing burning sensation in their bowels. The most sinful souls were completely reduced to ashes. Those who were guilty of lesser sins could enter heaven after making atonement, but they could never share all the pleasures of the most virtuous people. After several hours, the Master of Life ordered Lalawethika to return to earth to tell his people what he had learned and to urge them to repent of their evil doing.

Lalawethika began to weep as he completed his story. He vowed to renounce all his evil ways and said that his new name would be Tenskwatawa (the Open Door) to symbolize his role as a holy man who would lead his people to paradise. But he soon became known to the Americans and British simply as "The Prophet."

Many of The Prophet's teachings had to do with the decline of traditional values. He condemned violence. He admonished his listeners to treat elders with respect and to provide for kinsmen who were in need. He preached against polygamy and sexual promiscuity. He said that if Native people rejected the ways of white people and returned to the ways of their forefathers, the American Long Knives would be driven away and game would again be plentiful. Native people should reject "white" food such as wheat bread, beef, and pork, and they should only wear clothing made from leather and furs. He even told women who were married to white men that they should leave their husbands and their mixed-blood children.

He said that the Great Spirit had ordered him to found a separate community for believers where he should "instruct all from the different tribes that were willing to be good." As a result, in 1806 he formed a community called Prophet's Town, on the Tippecanoe River in Indiana. There he challenged the authority of Black Hoof and other leaders who opposed him. He accused them of being "very wicked" and of encouraging the people "in their former wicked ways."

One of the central tenets of The Prophet's teachings was opposition to witchcraft. He claimed that the Great Spirit had given him the power to discover witches, and he accused many people with political or religious ties to the Americans of being witches. Some of them he had killed.

Many people were skeptical of The Prophet, but others hoped that following his teachings would provide stability in their world — a world that was being altered by the large numbers of Long Knives moving into it. Prophet's Town grew rapidly as people from various tribes arrived to listen to The Prophet's message.

A Winnebago Legend

The Prophet gained so many followers among the Winnebago that a Winnebago legend grew up about him. According to this legend the Creator had fashioned him to accomplish a special mission on earth. The devil, in order to prevent Tenskwatawa from carrying out his mission, gave him a medicine belt that turned into a rattlesnake when he cast it on the ground. Under the devil's influence Tenskwatawa became a very wicked man who often got drunk and was feared by men and women alike. He was always surrounded by women because they were afraid not to do his bidding.

One night, while drunk, he was attacked by a group of men and nearly killed. The next day he decided to bathe in the river before taking his revenge on the men. While he was bathing a man came along and said to him, "I am sent to summon you, so let us go." The man took him to the Spirit Land. There the Creator asked Tenskwatawa if he was fulfilling the mission that he had received at his birth. Without waiting for an answer, the Creator showed him how deformed his body had become as a result of his bad behaviour. His mouth was twisted out of shape. His ears were so warped that it was a wonder that he could hear anything through them. His heart was rough and furrowed. The Creator then ordered him to return to earth and fulfill his mission.

When Tenskwatawa returned to earth, everyone scoffed at him and said that he was insane. Finally he fashioned a miniature war club and brought it to the assembly. He asked Tecumseh pick up the club, but he was unable to move it. Many other men also tried. Finally the people believed that Tenskwatawa was a prophet because he was the only one who was able to pick up the club.

The Second Confederacy
Tecumseh began to use The Prophet's message as a tool to

advance his political agenda of forming a new Native confederacy to replace the one destroyed by the Treaty of Greenville. He preached that all the lands in the Old Northwest belonged to a single Indian nation and that treaties negotiated with individual nations were invalid. He said that no individual had the right to sell their land, even to other Native peoples: "Sell a country! Why not sell the air [and] the great sea as well as the earth? Didn't the Great Spirit make them all for the use of his children?" On another occasion he remarked: "We gave them [the Long Knives] forest-clad mountains and valleys full of game. And in return what did they give our warriors and our women? Rum, trinkets and a grave."

Younger warriors tended to favour a confederacy, but many older chiefs were convinced that they had to seek accommodation with the Americans and adopt their ways in order to survive. Chief Black Hoof succeeded in keeping the majority of the Shawnee from supporting Tecumseh.

The Americans believed the confederacy was part of a British plot because the British government supported the Native desire for a separate state. The British, in fact, believed that a Native state would provide a useful buffer between the United States and Upper Canada.

Tecumseh's ambition was to prevent the loss of any more Native land to settlement, while William Henry Harrison's ambition was to open up enough land to white settlement so that Indiana could become a state. As a result, Harrison was on a collision course with Tecumseh from the moment he was elected governor of Indiana Territory in 1800.

Governor Harrison told the Indiana territorial legislature in 1806 that he had received "the most solemn assurances" from all the local tribes that they wished to maintain friendly relations with the United States. He said that the Native people would never have resorted to arms unless driven to it by injustice and oppression. Harrison admitted that Native complaints were "far from being groundless." Territorial laws provided equal punishment for offences committed against Indians and against whites, however, "The Indian always suffers, and the white man never." Harrison said he had received numerous complaints of white men hunting on Native lands and killing innocent Native people. One chief had complained that, should an Indian attempt to take a little bark from a tree to cover himself from the rain, "up comes a white man and threatens to shoot him, claiming the tree as his own."

In public, American president Thomas Jefferson appeared unconcerned about the influence of The Prophet. He wrote that there was little danger of his convincing many people to return to "the hardships and privations" of their traditional ways and "no great harm if he did." In private, however, Jefferson ordered Governor Harrison "to gain over The Prophet, who no doubt is a scoundrel and only needs his price."

Harrison called The Prophet a "fool who speaks not the words of the Great Spirit but those of the devil and of the British agents." Harrison sent a letter to the Shawnee in the name of the "Seventeen Fires" (the seventeen states making up the United States of America at that time), in which he implored them to drive The Prophet away if they valued the good opinion and friendship of the American government.

Harrison wrote to the Delaware, following the execution of a number of Delaware for witchcraft at the instigation of The Prophet:

> *[Is this pretended prophet] more wise or virtuous than yourselves that he should be selected to convey to you the orders of your God? Demand of him some proofs at least of his being the messenger of the Deity.... Ask of him to cause the sun to stand still, the moon to alter its course, the rivers to cease to flow, or the dead to rise from their graves."*

Unfortunately for Harrison, on June 16, 1806, shortly after he had sent that letter, there was an eclipse of the sun. Tecumseh had heard about the eclipse — possibly from a Canadian trader or from one of the scientists who had come to set up observation posts in the area — and suggested to The Prophet that they should invite all his followers to join them at Prophet's Town to see this great event. By the morning of June 16, Prophet's Town was crowded with visitors.

The sun rose as usual that morning, and everything remained normal until near midday. Then Tecumseh, looking through a piece of dark glass so that he could observe the eclipse without injuring his eyes, caught a glimpse of a dark line on the western edge of the sun. It was the edge of the moon. He told The Prophet, who raised his arms to the heavens and announced that he was about to make the sun disappear.

Gradually the moon covered the sun. The noonday heat began to lessen, and the sky took on a yellowish, unnatural colour. The crowd became uneasy. Children ceased playing and flocked around their mothers in terror. Men rejoined their families. Dogs cowered by their masters. Birds went to roost as if it were nightfall. Finally, the sky darkened sufficiently that stars came into view. The sun was almost completely obscured, although a corona of light was visible around it. After about three minutes light returned — not gradually, like a sunrise, but very suddenly. Everyone stood in awe, their faces turned upward, for several minutes after the light had returned.

The reputation of The Prophet was assured.

By the spring of 1807, American officials were very concerned about the large number of people assembled at Prophet's Town. President Jefferson sent a letter to Captain

Wells, the local Indian agent, informing him that Prophet's Town was on government land and ordering the residents to leave. Wells sent a messenger to invite Tecumseh and other leaders to come to Fort Wayne for discussions. Tecumseh was insulted and sent the messenger back to tell Captain Wells that, "if he has anything to communicate with me, he must come here; and I shall expect him six days from this time." Wells did not agree, and the situation remained quiet over the summer.

By fall, however, "reliable witnesses" testified that about one thousand people, in possession of new rifles from the British, had assembled in the area. Rifles were expensive at this time, and in reality only chiefs would likely have received them. Everyone else would have received muskets. The militia was called out and a government commission met with Native leaders at Chillicothe — likely the one in Ohio. Tecumseh made "an eloquent and masterly" speech that lasted three or four hours. He said that his people would remain peaceful if fairly treated, but they would also resist every attempt to settle on their lands. Some of the other men spoke, but it was evident that Tecumseh was their leader. The council ended amicably, with the government officials convinced that there was no immediate danger from the people gathered at Prophet's Town. The militia was disbanded.

Tecumseh Visits Upper Canada

In view of the increasing tension between the British and the Americans after 1805, Sir James Henry Craig, Governor-in-Chief of Upper Canada, began recruiting Indian allies. Craig said that if the British did not employ the Indians, "there cannot exist a moment's doubt that they will be employed against us."

In 1807 a clash between two naval frigates — the 38-gun American *Chesapeake* and the 50-gun British *Leopard* — increased fears of an American invasion of Upper Canada. Craig invited The Prophet to visit Upper Canada in 1808, suggesting to other officials that his influence be purchased "at what might be a high price upon any other occasion." Tecumseh, who was unknown to the Canadians and British at that time, arrived in his brother's place. Although Craig was impressed with Tecumseh, whom he described as "a very shrewd intelligent man," the British referred to him in their correspondence for some time to come as "Brother of The Prophet."

Tecumseh hated to be dependent on the British, especially after what he saw as their betrayal following the Battle of Fallen Timbers. He did realize, however, that a Native confederacy needed British support. He told the British that members of the confederacy had no intention in taking part in any war between the British and Americans, but "if their father the King should be in earnest and appear in sufficient force, they would hold fast by him."

William Claus had been deputy superintendent of the British Indian Department, which had been created in 1755 as a military organization to deal with relations between First Nations people and the government. Claus assembled chiefs at several key centres to consult with them, reminding them of the "artful and clandestine manner" in which the Americans had obtained their lands. Claus was so successful in his consultations that he had to restrain some chiefs from going to war immediately.

Although the British had lost the American Revolutionary War, they had an ongoing relationship with many of the Native peoples living on the American side of the border. The Americans were angry that the British Indian Department regularly issued gifts of ammunition and supplies to Native people on both sides of the border. The British claimed that the ammunition was for hunting, not for making war, and that without it many people might starve.

The British had also lost Detroit — their main fur-trading centre in the Upper Great Lakes — to the Americans by Jay's Treaty in 1796. They built Fort Amherstburg, about thirty five kilometres north, to replace Detroit, both as a military garrison and a headquarters for the Indian Department.

An Irishman named Isaac Weld Jr. described a gift-giving in the 1790s at Fort Amherstburg. On the appointed day, more than 400 people from a number of tribes were assembled. Each chief received a bundle of cedar sticks — long ones for warriors, medium ones for women and short ones for children — to keep track of how many people were in his group. Large stakes were fixed around the yard. Each stake was labelled with the name of a chief and the number of people eligible for gifts. The gifts included guns and ammunition, knives and hatchets, tobacco, and a variety of household goods.

It took several hours to distribute all the gifts. Afterwards, the commander of Fort Amherstburg told the assembled people that "their great and good father" (the king) who lived across the big lake (the Atlantic Ocean) was "ever attentive to the happiness of all his faithful people." He hoped that the young men would "have no occasion to employ their weapons in fighting against their enemies" and would use them only for hunting. He would send them more presents at the same time next year "if he still continued to find them good children."

As each paragraph was translated from English, the audience "signified their satisfaction" by exclamations of "Hoah! Hoah!" Each tribe then gathered up its gifts and departed "without speaking a word."

Chapter Three
Tecumseh's War

Their crimes are great
Our wrongs unspeakable! Yet my revenge
Is open war. It never shall be said
Tecumseh's hate went armed with cruelty.

Treaty of Fort Wayne

In the summer of 1809 The Prophet and about forty of his followers visited Governor Harrison at Vincennes, the capital of Indiana Territory. The Prophet declared that he had received and rejected an invitation from the British the previous fall to engage in a war against the Americans. He also said that he had convinced some tribes to abandon their hostility towards the Americans. Harrison, who did not believe The Prophet was sincere, wrote to the Secretary of War on July 5, informing him that the inhabitants of Prophet's Town were "a combination" that had been "produced by British intrigue and influence" in anticipation of a war between Britain and the United States.

In September, the chiefs of six neighbouring Nations — including the Delaware, the Miami and the Potawatomi — signed away about one million hectares of land to Governor

Harrison by the Treaty of Fort Wayne. The conflict that began at this time between Tecumseh and Harrison became known as Tecumseh's War.

The Miami had initially opposed signing the treaty, as young Miami warriors were constantly arriving home loaded with goods received from the British at Fort Amherstburg. Finally Harrison convinced them of the "perfidious conduct" of the British towards the Miami ever since the American Revolution. He said that the "present kindness" of the British was the result of a wish to embroil the Miami in conflict with the Americans in the event of war — because the British forces alone were not strong enough to defend Canada.

Although Tecumseh was furious when he learned the terms of the Treaty of Fort Wayne, he realized that direct military action against the Americans would be a mistake. It would likely cause the death of many Shawnee and the withdrawal of British support. As a result, he decided only to prevent the Americans from surveying the land and to threaten death to the "peace" chiefs who had signed the treaty.

The Prophet continued to accuse nonbelievers and political opponents of witchcraft. Wyandot chief Leatherlips, a major rival to Tecumseh, was put on trial and found guilty. A judge announced the verdict by handing Leatherlips a piece of birch bark with a hatchet drawn on it. Leatherlips accepted his sentence and calmly went to his execution singing his death song. Afterwards, the calumet and wampum belts that had been symbols of the first Native confederacy — which had officially ended with the treaty of Greenville — were transferred from the Wyandot town to Prophet's Town.

Meeting at Vincennes

Harrison, who was well aware of Tecumseh's opposition to the Treaty of Fort Wayne, sent him a letter in July 1810. The letter said that if the Shawnee could "show us the rightful owners of these lands which have been purchased," he would return the lands. He also offered to send Tecumseh and three other chiefs to Washington, if Tecumseh preferred to deal directly with the president.

Tecumseh set off for Vincennes to reply in person to Harrison's letter. He took with him a party of four hundred heavily armed warriors "painted in the most terrific manner." On their arrival they set up camp outside Vincennes, and Tecumseh — attended by fifteen or twenty warriors — approached the governor's mansion. Harrison and the other territorial officials were sitting on a platform on the lawn in front of the house. Harrison invited Tecumseh to take a seat with him, prefacing the invitation by saying that it was the wish of their "Great Father, the President of the United States" that he should do so.

Tecumseh didn't immediately reply. First he scanned the crowd. Then he fixed his eye on Harrison for a moment before raising one arm skyward. By this time, the crowd was silent and all eyes were fixed upon him. Finally, he exclaimed, "My Father? The sun is my father. The earth is my mother — and on her bosom I will recline." Then he and his men sat down on the lawn.

Harrison opened the council by asking Tecumseh if it was true that he had told the tribes who signed Treaty of Fort Wayne that they had no right to sell their land and that he had threatened to kill the chiefs who signed the treaty.

Tecumseh admitted he had done both these things and then stated at length his objections to the treaty. He said that the white men had driven his people from the seacoast, over the mountains, and were now pushing them into the lakes.

> *Now we are determined to go no farther.*
> *The only way to stop this evil is for all the*
> *red men to unite in claiming a common and*
> *equal right to the land ... Your states have*
> *set an example of forming a union ... [so]*
> *why should you censure the Indians for*
> *following that example?*

Tecumseh declined to visit the president until he had brought all the tribes together. He also charged that the Americans frequently broke the treaties they had made. He described one instance in which a Shawnee chief had been forced to sign a treaty that promised "if any white people mean to harm you, hold up these [American] flags and you will then be safe from all danger." Shortly afterwards, however, this same chief was murdered by an American officer as he stood with an American flag in front of him and a copy of a peace treaty in his hand. That officer was never punished.

Harrison rejected as "ridiculous" the idea that all Native people were one nation, arguing that the Great Spirit would have taught them all to speak the same language if he intended them to be one nation.

Tecumseh did not wait until the interpreter had finishing translating these words before breaking in angrily, "That is all false!" At that, his followers seized their weapons and sprang to their feet. Harrison immediately ordered his guards to advance. For a few minutes the two parties faced each other — warriors with hatchets and war clubs raised and guards with swords unsheathed and pistols cocked. Finally Harrison ordered Tecumseh to retire to his camp for the night. Tecumseh complied.

The following morning, Tecumseh sent an apology to Harrison and asked for another meeting. Harrison agreed. Tecumseh said that he had been encouraged to take a stand by two white men who had assured him that Harrison would soon be removed from office and that his replacement would restore the land to the Indians. He did not want to injure the governor, but he and his followers were determined to insist on the old boundary line and would prevent surveys of the land. Chiefs of five other Nations who were also present —

Wyandot, Kickapoo, Potawatomi, Ottawa, and Winnebago —
signified that they agreed with Tecumseh's stand.

Harrison promised to relay their claims to the American
president, but added that they might rest assured that
American title to these lands would be maintained by the
sword if necessary.

The council adjourned, but the following day Harrison
met with Tecumseh and an interpreter in private. Tecumseh
said that he did not want to go to war against the United
States. If the governor would persuade the president to give
up the land purchased by the Treaty of Fort Wayne and to
agree never to make another treaty without the consent of
all the tribes, Tecumseh promised that he would be a faithful
ally of the Americans. If the president refused, then he would
be compelled to become an ally of the British.

Harrison assured Tecumseh that his claims to the land
in question would never be acknowledged by the president.
Tecumseh responded:

> *I hope that the Great Spirit will put sense*
> *enough into his head to induce him to direct*
> *you to give up this land. It is true he is so*
> *far off he will not be injured by the war. He*
> *may sit still in his town, and drink his wine,*
> *while you and I will have to fight it out.*

Tecumseh pledged that in the event of war he would use

his influence to end cruelty to women, children and prisoners taken in conflict. The meeting broke up at that point.

Harrison sent an account of his meeting with Tecumseh to the American Secretary of War. Although he considered Tecumseh a threat to American interests, Harrison was very impressed with him as a leader. He wrote that the "obedience and respect" with which Tecumseh's followers treated him bespoke "him as one of those uncommon geniuses which spring up occasionally to produce revolutions." If Tecumseh were not so close to the United States, he might perhaps be the founder of "an empire that would rival Mexico or Peru."

Tecumseh's Visit to Fort Amherstburg

Following the Vincennes meeting Tecumseh made a second visit to Upper Canada. He travelled to Fort Amherstburg to meet with Colonel Matthew Elliott, who was superintendent of the British Indian Department from 1808 until his death in 1814. Tecumseh said that he had decided to throw in his lot with the British in a possible war with the Americans, because he wished to stop the Americans from taking up more Native land. Tecumseh then sent runners to inform other Indian nations of his support for the British. Twelve nations responded, sending more than five thousand people to Fort Amherstburg to seek alliance with the British. The British provided hunting equipment such as nets, traps, guns, and ammunition to the visitors.

Elliott, naturally, was delighted with the outcome of his meeting with Tecumseh and reported to colonial officials that Tecumseh had kept the Indians faithful and had shown himself "to be a determined character and a great friend to our Government."

The Americans, convinced that the Natives were being armed for war rather than for hunting, accused the British of meddling with internal American affairs.

Second Meeting at Vincennes

Harrison sent spies to Prophet's Town. They reported that The Prophet was very bitter towards the Americans and that many Indians had visited Fort Amherstburg. There, each warrior had received many gifts, including a good rifle and an abundance of ammunition. Harrison wrote to the War Department on July 3, 1811, that all the intelligence he had received confirmed the determination of The Prophet to commence hostilities against the United States as soon as he "thinks himself sufficiently strong." Harrison suggested that the best way to prevent war would be to send a force to disperse the "bandits."

Harrison also wrote to Tecumseh and his followers saying, you "threaten us with war ... I advise you to consider well of it ... Do you really think ... even that the whole of the tribes united could contend against the Kentucky Fire alone?" He again suggested that Tecumseh should lay his grievances before the president.

Tecumseh replied that he would go to Vincennes to talk to Harrison in person, just as he had the previous summer. Tecumseh arrived on July 27, with two to three hundred warriors. When a militia officer told Tecumseh that he could not enter Vincennes with so many men, Tecumseh left most of his force camped about a mile from the town. The townspeople were greatly alarmed, convinced that it was Tecumseh's intention to plunder the town. More companies of militia were called to the area.

After protracted negotiations Tecumseh and his immediate followers were finally admitted to the grounds of the governor's mansion. There they met with Harrison, who was attended by a troop of unmounted dragoons with pistols in their belts and carrying swords. Tecumseh's men were armed with clubs, hatchets, and knives. This meeting was no more successful than the previous one. Tecumseh told Harrison that he was going to meet with the Chickasaw, Choctaw, and Creek nations of the South. He expected to be gone almost a year and would meet with the president of the United States on his return. He requested, therefore, that Harrison not settle any of the territory acquired by the Treaty of Fort Wayne until after his return. Harrison, not surprisingly, did not agree.

The Battle of Tippecanoe

The bullets of the Long-Knives will rebound,
Like petty hailstones, from our naked breasts;
And in the misty morns of our attack,
Strange lights will shine on them to guide our aim,
Whilst clouds of gloom will screen us from their sight.

Harrison reported Tecumseh's proposed southern visit to the War Department and asked President Madison, who had replaced Jefferson in 1809, for permission to attack Prophet's Town on the Tippecanoe River while Tecumseh was absent. An added incentive for Harrison's attack was that one of Tecumseh's allies, Potawatomi Chief Main Poche (Withered or Black Hand), was attacking settlements in southern Illinois. In late September Harrison's forces set off for Prophet's Town. Along the way they met with the Delaware chiefs, who reported that The Prophet was making warlike preparations and that Shawnee warriors had severely wounded one of Harrison's sentinels ten days previously. Harrison sent a Delaware delegation to The Prophet with a list of demands, which included a requirement that all non-Shawnee people living in Prophet's Town should return to their own homes.

Before leaving for the south, Tecumseh had advised The Prophet not to do anything to provoke Harrison. Tecumseh still hoped that the Americans would negotiate with the

Native confederacy and that war would be avoided. In an attempt to satisfy both Tecumseh and the more aggressive of his followers, such as Main Poche, The Prophet vacillated between peace offerings and war threats as Harrison's army of some nine hundred or a thousand men approached. On November 6, Harrison's forces arrived near Prophet's Town.

The Prophet sent a delegation of three to meet Harrison. The delegation expressed surprise that the army seemed in such a haste to attack them, saying that the Delaware emissaries had told them that the army would not attack until The Prophet had responded to Harrison's demands. The delegation also claimed that The Prophet's response had not been delivered to Harrison, because the people delivering it had "searched for the army on the wrong side of the river." The two sides agreed to meet next morning. Harrison ordered his men to remain on the alert. They were to sleep within a few feet of their assigned battle positions with their arms at the ready. A large number of sentries patrolled the perimeter of the camp.

Shawnee chief White Loon later said that initially The Prophet, Wea chief Stone Eater, and he had intended to meet Harrison the following morning as they had promised. In early evening, however, Potawatomi chief Winnemac arrived and advised The Prophet that they should strike before dawn. The other leaders disagreed, but Winnemac finally prevailed. He called those who opposed him cowards and threatened to take his followers and return home. Since about one-third of the warriors were Potawatomi, the others were forced to agree to his plan.

The Prophet told his followers that the Great Spirit had instructed him that the warriors should strike before the next sunrise. He, The Prophet, would stand on a knoll near the battlefield, praying and chanting war songs that would make the warriors immune to the white man's bullets. The most important part of the plan was that Harrison should die.

Chiefs Winnemac, Stone Eater and White Loon were chosen as military leaders. They agreed that a group of a hundred warriors would crawl through the swamps on the northeast side of Harrison's camp before daylight, kill the sentries, sneak into the camp, and kill Harrison before attacking the camp as a whole. Harrison's company had lit large fires against the chill November night before bedding down. These fires created a serious problem for them when the camp was attacked in the predawn darkness. The troops were easy targets in the glow of the campfires, and many were shot as they tried to extinguish them.

The Prophet had told the warriors that as long as they heard him beat his drum they should continue fighting. The Indian pattern of attack was a series of local assaults in which warriors, yelling wildly, rushed a section of the camp perimeter. Each time they were driven back they quickly regrouped and rushed the line again. They were unusually aggressive, fired by The Prophet's promise that enemy bullets couldn't hurt them. As more warriors fell in battle, however, some men told The Prophet that his magic was failing. In the light of dawn they could see that Harrison was still alive, "riding fearlessly among his troops." As a result, they lost heart and soon after daylight Harrison's army routed them.

American Isaac Naylor, who participated in the Battle of Tippecanoe as a volunteer rifleman, wrote an account of the battle. The troops had set up camp about sunset. Harrison posted a strong guard around the encampment and ordered the men "to sleep on their arms." When Naylor woke at about 4 a.m. a drizzling rain was falling and all was quiet in camp. A few moments later he heard a rifle shot. At first he thought that one of the sentinels had fired his rifle without a real cause. Then he heard the crack of another rifle, followed by "an awful Indian yell." Immediately afterwards warriors charged the camp and shot a great many rifle balls into the campfires, throwing live coals into the air. A friend who had been sleeping across the campfire from Naylor was shot dead. The Indians made four or five such charges. At each charge they were driven back in confusion. Finally, just after daylight, they retreated across the prairie towards their town, carrying off their dead and wounded.

A different version of events was told by a Kickapoo chief who visited Colonel Elliott at Fort Amherstburg in

January 1812. The chief told Elliott that Harrison had arrived near Prophet's Town "without having sent any previous message," and with the intention of surrounding the village so that no one could escape. Overnight, Native pickets frequently encountered American "spies" and ordered them to return to their camp, without doing them any injury. Finally, two young Winnebago were wounded by American sentinels. When the sentinels came closer to finish them off, the Winnebago rose and tomahawked them. "This insult [the action of the sentinels] roused the indignation of the Indians and they determined to be revenged and accordingly commenced the attack at cock crowing." The Americans were caught between Winnebago and Kickapoo forces until about 9 a.m., when the Indians gave way "for want of arrows and ammunition." Elliott gathered that most of the Indians were more interested in plundering and stealing horses than in attacking the Americans, and that no more than 100 out of the two hundred and fifty to three hundred warriors present were engaged. About twenty-five of that number were killed.

Although Harrison felt his victory was decisive, he was incapable of taking full advantage of it. Nearly one-fifth of his men were dead or wounded, and they were low on rations. Thus they could not pursue the fleeing warriors. Instead, they gathered up food — more than five thousand bushels of corn and beans — and a cache of muskets and ammunition from the abandoned Prophet's Town before burning it and returning to Vincennes. Harrison considered the captured weapons proof of British assistance — possibly because they were marked with a British Government Board of Ordnance symbol. It is also possible that the warriors had not made full use of the available weapons, since The Prophet's teaching was to return to the old ways.

Two weeks after the battle, the area tribes arrived at Fort Wayne to receive the regular annuities they were entitled to by the Treaty of Fort Wayne. Harrison said that the President of the United States would only pardon members of those nations that had previously supported The Prophet when The Prophet and any of his followers who did not belong on the Wabash "were removed from the country."

Shawnee chief Black Hoof replied that they wished to live in peace and friendship with the Americans. The Prophet had been imprisoned by his disenchanted followers after Tippecanoe and many believed that he should be killed.

Chief Stone Eater, one of the leaders at Tippecanoe, led a delegation to meet with Harrison in early January. Stone Eater said that the Wea wished to re-establish friendship with the Americans. They no longer supported The Prophet, who had escaped after being in prison for two weeks. Stone Eater promised that they would punish The Prophet or deliver him to the Americans as soon as they could catch him.

The Prophet had lost virtually all of his influence, and only about forty Shawnee remained loyal to him.

Chapter Four
Prelude to the War of 1812

The distant tribes will unite with us
To spurn the fraudful treaties of Fort Wayne.
From Talapoosa to the Harricanaw
I have aroused them from their lethargy.

Three months before the Battle of Tippecanoe, and immediately after his meeting with Governor Harrison in August 1811, Tecumseh, accompanied by twenty well-armed warriors, left on his tour to meet with the southern tribes. Tecumseh and his men travelled down the Wabash River to the Mississippi, making their first stops with the Osage and the Chickasaw Nations.

Although Tecumseh would have preferred to remain independent of all white people, he realized that British support was essential to the Native cause in any war between the Americans and the British. As a result he told the Osage, "Our Great Father, over the great waters, is angry with the white people, our enemies. He will send his brave warriors against them; he will send us rifles, and whatever else we want — he is our friend, and we are his children."

Among the Chickasaw and Choctaw

Tecumseh had no success among the Chickasaw. They were at peace with the Americans and wished to remain so. As a result he quickly moved on to the village of noted Choctaw leader Hoentubbee, where he met with people from across the Choctaw Nation.

Hoentubbee described the appearance of Tecumseh and his party. All of the men wore their hair in three long braids down their backs but had their temples shaved. Their faces were painted with semicircular streaks of red war paint under each eye and a small red spot on each temple. They also each had a large red spot painted in the centre of their breast. While the other men wore hawk and eagle feathers in their hair, Tecumseh was adorned with two long crane feathers — one white, the other dyed a brilliant red. The white feather was an emblem of peace among the tribes. The red feather was an emblem of war with his enemies.

Tecumseh told the Choctaw that the white men were too strong for any one tribe alone to resist, and that many once-powerful tribes had already vanished "as snow before a summer sun." He painted a vivid picture of what would happen if the Choctaw did not unite with other tribes against their common enemies:

> *Soon your mighty forest trees, under the*
> *shade of whose wide spreading branches*
> *you have played in infancy, sported in*

boyhood, and now rest your wearied limbs
after the fatigue of the chase, will be cut
down to fence in the land which the white
invaders dare to call their own.... War or
extermination is now our only choice.

Chief Pushmataha replied to Tecumseh's speech. He agreed that the Choctaw had suffered great wrongs at the hands of the Americans, but he strongly disagreed with Tecumseh's solution to the problem. He said that going to war against the Americans — whose territories were far greater and who were far better armed than the Native peoples — would end in the total destruction of all of the tribes. Pushmataha was so adamant in his opposition that he threatened to put to death any Choctaw warrior who followed Tecumseh. He even threatened to kill Tecumseh if he did not leave Choctaw territory.

Meeting with the Creek

The annual grand council of the Creek Nation took place at the village of Tookabatcha during Tecumseh's visit there in October. An American general named Sam Dale, who apparently was present as a private citizen because he was curious to see what was going on, provided the following eyewitness account. Knowing that Tecumseh was to address the council, many more people than usual — an estimated five thousand — attended. On the day that Tecumseh spoke, he led his warriors into the centre of the town square in single file. They marched around the square three times, leaving a piece of tobacco at each corner. Next they circled the central flagpole three times and emptied their tobacco pouches on the small fire burning at the base of the pole. Only then did they approach Creek chief Big Warrior and his councillors. Tecumseh and each of the other Shawnee warriors greeted the Creek leaders with a war whoop before Tecumseh presented Big Warrior with a wampum belt. Tecumseh then produced his pipe, which was elaborately decorated with shells, beads, painted eagle feathers, and porcupine quills. Tecumseh lit the pipe and passed it to Big Warrior. Big Warrior solemnly took several puffs from the pipe before passing it around to his warriors.

At last, Tecumseh began to speak. He began slowly, but soon he was "hurling out his words like a succession of thunderbolts." Sometimes his voice sank to low and musical whispers; at other times it rose to the highest key. Dale wrote that he had heard many great orators, but "I never heard one with the vocal powers of Tecumseh, or the same command of the face. Had I been deaf, the play of his countenance would have told me what he said."

Dale claimed that he was able to repeat the very words of Tecumseh's speech. However, in view of the violent words against women and children, which he attributed to Tecumseh, Dale's accuracy is questionable. Tecumseh began by implying that he had killed some settlers as he travelled south through Ohio and Kentucky. Then he accused the Creek of cowardice because they did not wish to go to war against the Americans. He said that previously other tribes trembled to hear Creek war-whoops, and maidens from distant tribes sang songs of the prowess of Creek warriors and sighed for their embraces. "Now," he charged, "your very blood is white, your tomahawks have no edges, your bows and arrows were buried with your fathers." He concluded by saying that all white men should be driven back to the ocean that had first brought them to the red man's land.

> *Burn their dwellings! Destroy their stock!*
> *Slay their women and children! The red man*
> *owns the country, and the pale-face must*
> *never enjoy it.... Dig their very corpses*
> *from the graves! Our country must give no*
> *rest to a white man's bones.... All the tribes*
> *of the north are dancing the war dance. Two*
> *mighty warriors across the seas will send*
> *us arms.*

Tecumseh understood English and could speak enough to hold simple conversations, but he always spoke to officials through his interpreter in order to avoid being misunderstood. His translator during his Southern tour was a gifted linguist named Seekaboo, who was a distant relative.

The New Madrid Earthquake

As Tecumseh was leaving after his speech, he told the Creek that he could offer proof that the Great Spirit had sent him. He promised that when he arrived in Detroit he would stamp on the ground with his foot and shake down every house in the Creek village.

Two months later, on December 16, 1811, at precisely 2:30 a.m., the inhabitants of Tookabatcha were awakened by a mighty rumbling as a massive earthquake rocked the ground along the Mississippi River and destroyed their village. The quake was centred near New Madrid, which is located in present-day Missouri. It occurred on the very morning that Big Warrior estimated Tecumseh would arrive in Detroit. As a result, many of the Creek took up their weapons and prepared to go to war.

Several early historians claimed that Tecumseh "prophesied" the New Madrid Earthquake when he was trying to convince people that that they should join his confederacy. He told his audiences that when tribal unification was completed, a meteor would appear overnight on November 16 and exactly thirty days later the earth would tremble, great trees would fall without a wind storm, streams would change course, and lakes would suddenly appear or disappear. On that day all the tribes would be united and they would be able to regain their lost land. Immediately after that, the people were all to assemble in one place — variously listed as

Detroit, Vincennes or Tippecanoe. The Great Comet of 1811 (visible to the naked eye for nine months) was at its brightest in the middle of Tecumseh's southern trip, and the New Madrid Earthquake certainly did occur; therefore it seems quite likely that historians of the time concocted the prophesy story to fit with these facts.

Tragic Homecoming

When Tecumseh returned home that winter and learned about the events at Tippecanoe he was devastated. His confederacy had suffered an almost fatal blow with the destruction of Prophet's Town, and Tecumseh was so furious with The Prophet that he threatened to kill him. Tecumseh visited Governor Harrison and told him that he now wished to accept the invitation that Harrison had previously extended to him to visit the president. He wanted to tell the president that he would support the Americans if they agreed to recognize the confederacy. Harrison refused to agree to the trip when Tecumseh insisted that he would only travel to Washington accompanied by a large number of his warriors.

Both Tecumseh and The Prophet said that they objected to annuities, apparently because annuities were given for signing the treaties, which they so strongly opposed. Tecumseh also refused gifts from Harrison, telling him on one occasion that if he accepted presents, "you will hereafter say that with them you purchased another piece of land from us."

Despite these words, immediately after leaving Harrison, Tecumseh went to Fort Wayne to ask for lead and powder. When officials at Fort Wayne turned him down, he said that he would go to Fort Amherstburg instead and get ammunition from the British. The Americans warned him that this would be considered "an act of enmity," but they made no effort to stop him because they simply wanted the Native peoples to remain neutral.

Beginning in the early spring, small parties of Tecumseh's followers began to attack settlers on the frontier. Governor Harrison requested permission from the Secretary of War to raise a mounted force to punish the attackers, but permission was denied because the government feared that such action would drive Tecumseh and his followers into a closer relationship with the British.

Events in Upper Canada

General Isaac Brock, who would become one of the greatest British heroes of the War of 1812, was named military commander of Upper Canada in 1810. He wrote to the commander at Fort Amherstburg that military officials were not to interfere at any Native council other than "by being present." They should, however, "report confidentially" what might pass at those councils.

Brock also asked Indian Department staff to exert all their influence to prevent Native attacks on the American frontier, but he quickly realized that the latter task was nearly impossible because the Natives felt that they had been sacrificed after the Battle of Fallen Timbers.

The situation continued to deteriorate over the next few months. Both the British and the Americans, by combining shows of force with gift-giving, tried to gain Native support in any upcoming war. In February 1812 Brock wrote that the Americans were busy raising forces "for the express purpose of overawing the Indians" and that intrigues were being openly carried on among various tribes to gain their support. Brock expected the Americans to be successful in sowing divisions among "our Native allies and estranging the minds of many from our interests." He strongly advocated that the restrictions placed on the Indian Department be lifted. He said that each additional day that Indian Department officers advised peace and withheld the accustomed supply of ammunition, their influence over the Native people would diminish, till at length it would be lost altogether.

Tecumseh travelled to Upper Canada from Fort Wayne early in 1812 and met secretly with an Indian Department employee, who promised British aid to the confederacy. Tecumseh also delivered a speech at Amherstburg in reply to a message he had received from Colonel Elliott of the Indian Department. In this speech (recorded in Sir Isaac Brock's published correspondence) he blamed the Potawatomi for the Battle of Tippecanoe. He said that the Potawatomi had killed some of the Long Knives instead of listening "to our repeated counsel to remain quiet and live in peace" with them. Tecumseh continued:

> *If we hear of the Big Knives coming*
> *towards our villages to speak peace, we*
> *will receive them, but if we hear of any of*
> *our people being hurt by them ... we will*
> *defend ourselves like men. If we hear of any*
> *of our people having been killed, we will*
> *immediately send to all the Nations on or*
> *towards the Mississippi and all ... will rise*
> *as one man.*

It is unclear whether Tecumseh made this speech before or after attending the council at Mississinewa in mid-May.

Grand Council of Mississinewa

Twelve Indian nations met at a grand council at Mississinewa, near Fort Wayne, in mid-May to discuss the impending war. The majority opinion was in favour of keeping the peace with the Americans, and many councillors urged Tecumseh to restrain his young warriors, lest all the tribes suffer at the hands of the whites. A Wyandot orator said that the British supported Wyandot peace efforts and advised "all the red people to be quiet and not meddle in quarrels that may take place between the white people."

Tecumseh again blamed the Potawatomi, asserting that no blood would have been shed at Tippecanoe if he had been at home. A Delaware speaker said that it was too late to be blaming each other for what had happened and that "both red and white people have felt the bad effects" of The Prophet's counsel. He urged them to "join our hearts and hands together and proclaim peace through the land of the red people." The Miami agreed that to go to war with the whites would bring about their immediate ruin.

Tecumseh likely returned to Amherstburg immediately after leaving Mississinewa because he arrived there with about a hundred and fifty other Shawnee in early summer, 1812. According to a journal kept by William Hamilton Merritt, who fought on the British side during the War of 1812, Tecumseh soon gained the support of enough men from other tribes to form a force of between five and six hundred warriors. Merritt wrote:

> *Self-preservation is alone a sufficient plea for our having recourse to the assistance of these warriors.... The natives had commenced hostilities against the whites some time since, and certainly every candid and unbiased person must say they had sufficient reasons for doing [so], by the settlers unwarrantable encroachments on their lands and property. Every friend of humanity must deprecate the savage mode*

of warfare: to alleviate and restrain...
as much as possible, a grand council
of war was held at Amherstburg, where
their chiefs solemnly promised to abolish
the shocking practice of scalping, likewise
to save all prisoners that should fall into
their possession.

Chapter *Five*
War is Declared

Don't underrate his power! But for our States
This man would found an empire ...
Allied with England, he is to be feared
More than all other men.

American President James Madison formally declared war against Great Britain on June 18, 1812. Communications in North America, however, were so poor at the time that many people — including some members of the military — did not learn that they were at war for several weeks. The case of Brigadier General William Hull was particularly embarrassing for the Americans. Hull had been ordered to Detroit by the War Department in a dispatch written on the same day that war was declared, but the dispatch omitted to mention that important piece of information. It was not until July 2 that a courier caught up with Hull and delivered a second message informing him that the Americans and the British were at war. This message ordered Hull to proceed as quickly as possible to Detroit, where he was to make "such arrangements for the defence of the country as in your judgment may be necessary, and wait for further orders."

Hull had sent the schooner *Cuyahoga* on ahead to

The meeting of Brock and Tecumseh, by C. W. Jefferys, ca. 1921.

Detroit. It carried his trunk, which contained sensitive military and personal papers, as well as most of his troops' luggage and stores. A number of sick soldiers and some officers' wives were also on board. The same day that the courier caught up to Hull, the British captured the *Cuyahoga*. They forwarded Hull's trunk to General Brock, who soon received a rather petulant letter from Hull requesting that, "in the interest of fair play and good sportsmanship," his personal papers be returned, since he hadn't known that war had been declared. The officers' wives and military band instruments were returned to Detroit immediately, but apparently Brock kept Hull's papers.

The Americans first entered British territory on July 12, when Hull crossed the Detroit River and landed near Sandwich (now Windsor, Ontario) with two thousand men. The first engagements of the war on Canadian soil were a couple of skirmishes at the bridge over Rivière aux Canards near Amherstburg on July 16 and 24. During one of these skirmishes a British picket, which included soldiers from the 41st Regiment, militia and Tecumseh's warriors, was guarding the bridge. The Americans chased the picket away, but they could not hold the bridge. According to a history of the 41st Regiment, one of its own men, Private Hancock, was the first casualty of the war. The next day the American line gave way and the men retreated in confusion, pursued by the warriors. The Americans suffered six killed and two wounded.

The Battle of Maguaga

By early August, General Hull's army at Detroit was short of supplies, and Hull sent out an urgent request for help. The governor of Ohio responded by sending out a wagon train of supplies along with a hundred head of cattle on the hoof. The train was manned by nearly three hundred volunteers commanded by Captain Henry Brush. For much of the journey to Detroit, the men had to cut a new road through dense woods and marshy areas for the heavily loaded wagons and the cattle. Scouts reported the supply train to Colonel Henry Proctor at Fort Amherstburg. Proctor sent out a small detachment of regular soldiers, along with seventy warriors under the command of Tecumseh, to intercept the train.

Brush heard rumours about the impending attack, so he sent word to Detroit requesting an escort. On August 9, near the Native village of Maguaga (twenty-two kilometres below Detroit), the escort that had been sent to meet Brush blundered into an ambush set by Captain Adam Muir's detachment of a hundred and fifty British regulars and Canadian militia plus an unknown number of warriors led by Tecumseh. The Americans succeeded in beating back the ambush. However, the numbers of dead and wounded were high on both sides. As a result, after a night spent without food or shelter in the pouring rain, Hull ordered the whole detachment to return to Detroit. It was harassed along the way by gunfire from two boats on the Detroit River, so Hull decided that all his forces in Upper Canada should return to Detroit immediately.

Major John Richardson, who fought in the War of 1812 with the British 41st Regiment, wrote about the Battle of Maguaga and what he saw as the extreme disadvantages faced by regular British troops when fighting against Native warriors and American frontiersmen in the woods. According to Richardson the first disadvantage was the conspicuous dress of the English soldier as compared to Native dress. The second was the British officers' "utter ignorance of a mode of warfare in which courage and discipline are of no avail." Richardson thought that Maguaga offered "the most convincing proofs that without the assistance of the Indian warriors," the defence of much of Canada would have "proved a duty of great difficulty and doubt."

Many people today would disagree with Richardson's assessment of the relative abilities of British soldiers as opposed to Native warriors and frontiersmen. Ron Dale, a Canadian historian with a special knowledge of the War of 1812, claims that Richardson's views were completely wrong. He says that British light infantry could dress inconspicuously and fight quite successfully in heavy woods if need be. In most cases, however, the British wanted to be conspicuous. Because they were among the best-trained soldiers in the world, their red coats were very intimidating. Dale also gives more credit to the regular army than to the militia in winning battles.

Of the warriors in battle, Richardson wrote that they stained and painted their bodies "in the most frightful manner" — some white, some black, others half black and half red. They wore only a breechcloth, but were "armed to the teeth" with rifles, tomahawks, war clubs and scalping knives. They uttered no sound, "intent only on reaching the enemy unperceived."

The Sac chief Black Hawk likely spoke for many chiefs when he criticized the military tactics used by the British. "Instead of stealing upon each other, and taking every advantage to kill the enemy and save their own people, as we do … they march out in open daylight and fight, regardless of the number of warriors they may lose." Chief Black Hawk was expressing the difference in philosophy between a belief in the sanctity of the individual held by many First Nations societies and the European concept of acceptable losses.

Fort Dearborn Massacre

The Potawatomi had not been pleased when Fort Dearborn (now the city of Chicago) was built in the heart of their territory in 1803. "We looked upon the fort as a dangerous enemy within our camp," wrote Simon Pokagon, whose father, Leopold, was chief at the time. The defeat at Tippecanoe added to their anger against the Americans. So it is not surprising that the young warriors listened sympathetically when emissaries arrived in the early summer of 1812 to try to persuade the Potawatomi to support the British against the Americans.

On August 1, a fur trader arrived at Fort Dearborn to report that Fort Mackinac, at the northern end of Lake Huron, had surrendered to a combined force of British soldiers and Tecumseh's warriors, and that Fort Detroit would likely share the same fate — leaving Fort Dearborn as the only remaining American stronghold in the Northwest. The trader advised the Potawatomi "to sound at once the war whoop and besiege" Fort Dearborn. On August 7, dispatches from General Hull arrived at Fort Dearborn, suggesting that the fort be evacuated and that any unneeded supplies be distributed to the local Potawatomi people. Although most of his officers advised against such a move, fort commander Captain Nathan Heald decided to evacuate. Heald argued that the distribution of goods would please the Potawatomi and ensure that the garrison would reach Fort Wayne safely.

Heald called the Potawatomi to council and told them that he planned to evacuate the fort the next day on orders from General Hull. Heald promised them supplies and payment of a large sum of money if they would escort the garrison safely to Fort Wayne. The Potawatomi happily agreed and immediately received some supplies. That same night, however, Heald ordered all excess firearms, ammunition, and whiskey dumped into Lake Michigan. The Potawatomi were furious when they found out. They were even more furious when twenty Miami arrived at Fort Dearborn to escort the garrison to Fort Wayne. The Potawatomi naturally believed that Heald was not going to keep any part of his agreement with them.

On the morning of August 15, some one hundred soldiers and their families who lived in Fort Dearborn marched off to Fort Wayne. Potawatomi warriors ambushed them about three kilometres south of the fort. Casualties were very high on both sides, as were acts of barbarous behaviour. Simon Pokagon charged that "the pride of the white man" may disguise the fact, but "when he joins hands with untutored savages in warfare he is a worse savage than they." He also wrote that the English generals had formed a league with Tecumseh and his warriors to take the forts around the Great Lakes, regardless of consequences.

Tecumseh and General Brock Meet
General Isaac Brock arrived at Fort Amherstburg just before midnight on August 13 with a combined force of militia and regulars from the 41st Regiment. As they arrived, they heard the sound of musketry coming from an island in the Detroit River. Colonel Elliott explained that the firing came from their Indian allies, who were expressing their joy at the arrival of reinforcements. Brock, knowing how scarce munitions were, asked Elliott to ask the warriors to stop shooting and to promise them

that he (Brock) would speak to them the next morning. Elliott returned about half an hour later, bringing Tecumseh with him. Brock and Tecumseh shook hands and spoke briefly before agreeing to meet in council in the morning.

Brock's aide-de-camp described Tecumseh's appearance as "prepossessing." He was fairly tall, with a slim and well-proportioned figure, a light copper complexion and bright hazel eyes. Three small silver crowns hung from the lower cartilage of his aquiline nose, and a large silver medallion of George III hung around his neck. He wore plain deerskin jacket and trousers, their seams covered with a neatly cut fringe. On his feet he wore moccasins, much ornamented with dyed porcupine quills.

The council opened precisely at noon. Brock, surrounded by his officers, took his stand beneath a giant oak. Tecumseh sat directly in front of Brock, with his fellow chiefs ranged behind him. Behind them were a thousand warriors in full war paint. Brock told the assembled group that the Long Knives had come to take away the land of both the Indians and the British in Canada:

> *I have fought against the enemies of our great father, the king, beyond the great lake, and they have never seen my back. I am come here to fight his enemies on this side [of] the great salt lake, and now desire with my soldiers to take lessons from you and*

*your warriors, that we may learn how to
make war in these great forests.*

At the end of Brock's speech, there was a short pause. Tecumseh then turned to his warriors, stretched out his hand and said, "This is a man!"

The warriors loudly applauded, and Tecumseh was called on to reply. He said that his people were very happy that their father beyond the great salt lake had finally "awoke from his long sleep" and allowed his warriors to come to the assistance of his Native children. Tecumseh pledged that his people were ready "to shed their last drop of blood in their great father's service."

When the council broke up, Brock invited Tecumseh and several other leading warriors to meet privately with him and his senior officers. Brock explained to them in detail how he planned to attack Fort Detroit. Tecumseh assured Brock that he and his fellow warriors unanimously agreed to the plan and that their complete cooperation could be depended upon. Brock, who was unfamiliar with the countryside, asked Tecumseh to describe it to him. Tecumseh unrolled a piece of bark and anchored it to the ground with stones at each corner. Then, with the point of his knife, he carefully marked the positions of roads and natural features to form an accurate map of the area.

The Fall of Detroit

Before launching his attack on Detroit, Brock formally demanded in writing that Brigadier General Hull surrender the fort:

> *The force at my disposal authorizes me to require of you the immediate surrender of Fort Detroit. It is far from my intention to join in a war of extermination; but you must be aware that the numerous body of Indians who have attached themselves to my troops will be beyond my control the moment the contest commences.*

When Hull refused to surrender, Brock launched an immediate assault. He ordered a battery of five guns at Sandwich, directly across the river from Detroit, to open fire. The Americans countered by firing their battery of seven 24-pounders back across the river at the British. The distance was too great for either battery to do much damage, so Brock soon ordered his men to cease fire. They retired to their bivouac with orders to sleep on their arms and to cross the river at dawn the next morning.

That night, under cover of darkness, a force of five or six hundred warriors silently crossed the river in a flotilla of canoes. Led by Tecumseh and Colonel Elliott, they crept ashore and stole soundlessly on moccasined feet into the dense forest surrounding Fort Detroit. Hull's anxious sentries did not realize that some of the bird cries they heard were actually signals being passed from warrior to warrior.

As dawn broke about 4 a.m., Brock led his army across the river. Well covered by a small armed boat and the shore batteries, they landed without opposition below Detroit. Brock organized his men in columns and ordered them to march twice as far apart as normal from each other. As Brock came into range of the fort's heaviest guns — about 2.5 kilometres — he led his men into a nearby ravine. Immediately, the sound of war whoops came from the woods, and Tecumseh paraded his warriors across the field in view of the fort. They disappeared into the forest again and doubled back to where they had started their march. According to one — probably apocryphal — story, they did this a number of times, convincing Hull that he was facing a force of fifteen hundred warriors.

Brock credited the dressing of the militia in cast-off scarlet military uniform coats as a crucial factor in winning the battle. As the army neared Sandwich each volunteer was placed between two regular soldiers. One man later recalled that Brock gave the following order to the volunteers: "If your lieutenant falls, take his place; if your captain falls, take his place; if your colonel falls, take his place."

Hull was also misled as to the size of the force against him by a phony letter sent by one British officer to another.

The first officer wrote the second officer that he need not send down more than five thousand warriors to capture Detroit because he (the writer) already had a considerable force of regular soldiers. This letter was deliberately let fall into Hull's hands, giving him visions "of an overwhelming force coming down upon his rear, while a superior army should attack him in front."

Just as Brock was about to launch an assault on the fort, Hull hoisted a white flag in immediate surrender. Everyone was shocked. Hull likely would not have surrendered if he had known that half of Brock's force were militia, but he assumed that Brock's regulars would capture the fort and that the Native allies would massacre its inhabitants after the battle was over. The warriors marched out of the woods, yelling and firing their muskets in the air in celebration. Tecumseh and Brock, both astride impressive grey horses, watched from in front of the British line while the British colours replaced the American flag over the fort. Brock publicly honoured Tecumseh by presenting him with his own pistols and crimson sash, which he personally tied about Tecumseh's waist. Tecumseh, in his turn, presented his multicoloured arrow-patterned sash to Brock, who wore it until the day he died.

The day following the surrender, Tecumseh was seen without Brock's sash. When asked where it was, Tecumseh replied that he had given it to Wyandot chief Roundhead because he, Tecumseh, did not feel entitled to wear such a mark of distinction when an older and abler warrior was present.

As a result of Hull's surrender, his whole army were taken prisoners of war, Michigan Territory became a military possession of Britain, and an abundance of food and military stores fell into British hands. After the fall of Detroit, Brock wrote that the conduct of the Indians and the chiefs of their respective tribes were "marked with acts of true heroism." He also praised Native treatment of prisoners in a letter to the Governor General of Upper Canada, saying that they treated the prisoners "with every humanity." A few days later, Brock wrote that of all the Native people he met at Amherstburg, he was most impressed with Tecumseh. "A more sagacious or ... gallant warrior does not, I believe, exist."

Although neither Brock nor Hull knew it at the time, Governor General George Prevost of Upper Canada had negotiated a one-month truce with the Americans the week before the capture of Fort Detroit. Brock and Tecumseh were furious when they learned about the armistice, because it gave the Americans time to reinforce their armies. Tecumseh asked Brock to pledge his word that England would enter into no negotiations in which Native interests were not included. Brock agreed, and over the next month or two he tried to undo the harm he felt had been caused by the truce. He wrote that the Native allies were extremely suspicious of British conduct. If they became convinced that the British lacked the means to prosecute the war vigorously or were negotiating a separate peace, Brock believed they would immediately begin to plan how "they can most effectually deceive us." Brock told British officials that losing Tecumseh's support could prove fatal to the war effort and reminded them of their promise to support a Native confederacy south of the Great Lakes. Brock charged that the American government had corrupted a few dissolute characters "whom they pretended to consider as chiefs" and concluded treaties with them that they were attempting to impose on the whole Indian race.

General Brock was killed at the Battle of Queenston Heights in October 1812, almost two months to the day after the capture of Detroit. He was knighted posthumously. Despite such horrific events as those that had already occurred at Fort Dearborn, and were about to occur at Raisin River, the official document accompanying Brock's honour praised the Native forces who served under him. It stated that the cooperation of the Indian nations "has been marked by steadiness and order, and that they treated their prisoners with humanity."

Chapter Six
Raisin River to the Battle of Lake Erie

And every tongue cries for our children's land
To expiate their crime of being born.
Oh, we have ever yielded in the past,
But we shall yield no more! ...
Let not the Long-Knife build one cabin there —
Or fire from it will spread to every roof,
To compass you, and light your souls to death.

At dawn on a frosty morning in late January 1813, an event took place that outraged the American public.

Previously, the residents of Frenchtown (present-day Monroe, Michigan), on the Raisin River, had asked for help because their hamlet had been occupied by British forces and their Native allies. Brigadier General James Winchester, with a force of untrained Kentucky frontiersmen, came to their aid and dispersed a small British detachment on January 18. When British commander Colonel Henry Proctor learned of this, he quickly ordered a counterattack by his own troops and warriors led by Wyandot chiefs Roundhead and

Walk-in-the-Water. They travelled over the river ice, bringing artillery and about thirteen hundred men.

Their arrival at Frenchtown surprised the American force, who were still asleep in their bedrolls. Although the Americans quickly took up their positions and returned fire, they were outnumbered and soon forced to retreat. After recapturing Frenchtown, Proctor immediately withdrew. He didn't have enough sleighs to transport the wounded, so he left five hundred prisoners guarded by his Native allies. The captured Kentucky frontiersmen were bitter enemies of the warriors, and without Tecumseh present to maintain order the Wyandot executed between thirty and sixty prisoners.

This event, which the American press called the "River Raisin Massacre," greatly aided militia recruitment. "Remember the River Raisin" became the rallying cry of an outraged American public.

The chiefs had solemnly promised at the beginning of the war to "alleviate and restrain" the practice of taking scalps, but it quickly became evident that not only warriors were guilty of such cruelty. In the first skirmish of the war, at Rivière aux Canards, a warrior was killed and scalped by an American officer. That officer was in turn killed and scalped at Brownstown shortly afterwards. The chiefs then called a council at which they produced the officer's body and retracted all former promises regarding scalps.

Sieges of Forts Meigs and Stephenson

On April 23, 1813, Proctor set off by boat to attack Fort Meigs, on the south bank of the Maumee River. His force included about a thousand soldiers plus twelve hundred warriors led by Tecumseh and Wyandot chief Roundhead. On April 28 they established their main camp near the ruins of British Fort Miami on the north bank of the Maumee River, ten kilometres downstream from Fort Meigs. Proctor and Tecumseh made a reconnaissance mission on horseback along the river to a high piece of land opposite Fort Meigs. They decided to place two batteries there and immediately sent out a fatigue party under the command of the Royal Engineers to begin construction. When the Americans saw the batteries going up they responded by constructing an earthen wall for protection — after first erecting tents to hide their activity from the British. Despite incessant rains and the wretched condition of the roads, the British batteries were operational by May 1. One battery held two 24-pounders; the other, three howitzers.

It was not until the British began to fire their guns that they realized what the Americans had done. Proctor wrote that the Americans had "so completely entrenched" themselves as to "render unavailing every effort of our artillery," despite the batteries' being judiciously placed and well constructed.

Then, on May 5, more than twelve hundred Kentucky

militiamen arrived as reinforcements and attacked the British on both sides of the river. The enemy briefly gained possession of the British batteries and took some prisoners. After a short but severe fight the British, under the command of Major Adam Muir, routed the Americans. Proctor said that he didn't know how many prisoners the warriors had taken in the May 5 fight, but he had returned five hundred prisoners to the Americans. He speculated that between a thousand and twelve hundred Americans had been killed or taken prisoner.

The day after the battle, however, Proctor was forced to lift the siege because half of the Canadian militia had left and the remainder threatened to leave. Most were farmers who wanted to return home for spring seeding. The chiefs advised him that they also could not prevent their people from leaving. It was their custom, after any battle of consequence, to return home with their wounded, their prisoners and their plunder. "Before the ordnance could be withdrawn, I was left with Tecumseh and less than twenty chiefs and warriors," Proctor commented ruefully, although he hastened to add that he had subsequently brought all the ordnance safely away.

Several other sources give more details about the Siege of Fort Meigs. When the British discovered that the American fortifications had rendered their batteries ineffective, a force led by Muir and Tecumseh crossed the river, protected by gunboats, and erected a small secondary battery on the edge of a ravine, three hundred metres from the fort. Under the command of Colonel William Dudley, eight hundred of the American militiamen who had arrived on May 5 were ordered to attack the main British batteries. Dudley's force quickly captured the guns. However, they disregarded the second part of their orders, which were to return to the fort immediately afterwards. Instead, they engaged in a skirmish with Tecumseh's men. As Tecumseh lured most of them into the woods, the 41st Regiment recaptured the batteries and a few militiamen who had remained there.

Of Dudley's eight hundred men, barely a hundred and fifty managed to return safely to Fort Meigs. They had pursued the warriors almost to the British camp before the warriors attacked. Many militiamen were taken prisoner. Others, including Dudley, were massacred in full view of British officers, who made no attempt to stop the warriors.

When Tecumseh learned what was happening, he rushed to the scene, raised his hatchet and threatened to destroy the first man who did not obey his order to stop killing the prisoners. Tecumseh then demanded to know why Proctor had not put a stop to the killing. Proctor's excuse was that he believed the warriors were running amok and were beyond his control. The outraged Tecumseh replied, "You are unfit to command; go and put on petticoats."

Despite Tecumseh's poor opinion of Proctor, he tried

to persuade the colonel to make a second attempt against Fort Meigs shortly afterwards. Finally, in mid-July, after many warriors had returned to the area, Proctor agreed.

Tecumseh proposed a plan for taking the fort. The warriors would land several kilometres below the fort and secretly travel through the woods to an area nearby where they would engage in a mock battle. Tecumseh anticipated that the garrison commander would believe reinforcements were being attacked on their way to the fort and would immediately send his men out to defend them. The warriors would then ambush these defenders and gain entrance before the gates could be secured against them.

On July 25, Tecumseh put his plan into action. The sounds of the mock battle convinced almost everyone in the garrison — except for the commander — that it was a genuine attack. Despite the fact that the other officers demanded permission to lead a rescue mission, the commander refused to allow his men to leave the fort. As a result of the failure of Tecumseh's plan, the British withdrew three days later.

Many warriors left for home, but those remaining were anxious to attack the nearby Fort Stephenson. Proctor agreed and arrived at the fort on August 1, with about four hundred members of the 41st Regiment and several hundred warriors. Tecumseh and almost two thousand more warriors were stationed on the roads leading to Fort Stephenson, to prevent American reinforcements from reaching the fort. On the

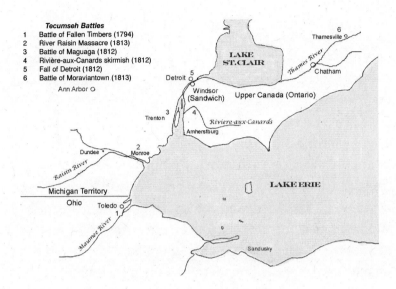

Tecumseh Battles
1 Battle of Fallen Timbers (1794)
2 River Raisin Massacre (1813)
3 Battle of Maguaga (1812)
4 Rivière-aux-Canards skirmish (1812)
5 Fall of Detroit (1812)
6 Battle of Moraviantown (1813)

Tecumseh Battles Map, by Donald L. Gordon.

afternoon of August 2, the British redcoats advanced against two sides of the fort. According to Proctor, his troops "displayed the greatest bravery," but the warriors had "scarcely come into fire before they ran off out of its reach." Proctor, after losing ninety-six men, called off the assault. Governor General Prevost wrote a letter to Proctor on August 22, criticizing him for allowing "the clamour of the Indian warriors to induce you to commit a part of your valuable force in an unequal and hopeless conflict."

Although the defeat at Fort Stephenson was partially due to the warriors' failure to fight, both militia and warriors faulted Proctor's tactics. Tecumseh also later admitted to Proctor that his warriors had provided little assistance because "It is hard to fight people who live like groundhogs," although it is unclear which of the 1813 sieges Tecumseh was referring to in this comment.

The Beginning of the End

In June 1813 Proctor was short of supplies and desperately in need of seamen to defend Lake Erie. Fort George had been captured by the Americans on May 27, disrupting the normal supply route along the Niagara Portage to Lake Erie. Also, the depot at Fort York had been captured, Fort Malden was cut off and the American squadron had the upper hand on Lake Ontario. Proctor said that a reliable regular force and the delivery of more food would encourage his Indian allies. The current shortage of food meant that many warriors might desert unless they were very strongly in support of the British cause.

By September Amherstburg was threatened with starvation. The Americans had constructed a fleet on Lake Erie over the winter of 1813 — although it was not launched until later in the summer — and the British had to remove this threat before they could retrieve supplies from a depot at the eastern end of the lake. On September 10, 1813, the British suffered a serious naval defeat at the hands of the American flotilla. Commonly known as the Battle of Lake Erie, it is also sometimes referred to as the Battle of Put-in-Bay, since it took place near the bay of that name in Ohio.

After the defeat, Proctor ordered the destruction of Amherstburg, rather than let it fall into American hands, and tried unsuccessfully to conceal news of the American victory from Tecumseh. Tecumseh had already concluded that Proctor was both incompetent and a coward, and guilty of "numerous falsehoods." For example, when Proctor began preparing to retreat from Fort Amherstburg, he initially told Tecumseh that he was only sending valuables up the Thames River for safety.

Finally Tecumseh had had enough. He angrily confronted Proctor, reminding him of the promises made by the British:

> *When war was declared, our father...*
> *told us that he was now ready to strike*
> *the Americans — that he wanted our*
> *assistance; and that he would certainly*
> *get us our lands back... You told us at that*
> *time to bring forward our families to this*
> *place ... and you promised to take care of*
> *them... while the men would go and fight*
> *the enemy ... We are much astonished to see*
> *our father... preparing to run away ... We*
> *must compare our father's conduct to a fat*
> *animal that carries its tail upon its back, but*
> *when affrighted, drops it between its legs*
> *and runs off.*

*...The Americans have not yet defeated
us by land; neither are we sure that they
have done so by water; we therefore wish
to remain here, and fight our enemy ... If
they defeat us, we will then retreat with
our father ... You have got the arms and
ammunition which our great father sent for
his red children. If you have any idea of
going away, give them to us, and you may
go in welcome ... Our lives are in the hands
of the Great Spirit. We are determined to
defend our lands, and if it is his will, we
wish to leave our bones upon them.*

When Tecumseh had completed his speech, the other
warriors brandished their hatchets menacingly and loudly
approved his sentiments. Tecumseh suggested that, rather
than retreating, they should allow the Americans to land and
move towards Amherstburg. Tecumseh's force would then
attack the American flank and rear, while Proctor and his regulars and militiamen would assail them from the front. If the
Americans did capture Fort Amherstburg, Tecumseh would
then make a stand at Rivière aux Canards, site of the first
skirmish of the war. Although Proctor did not defend himself
against Tecumseh's angry speech, he did reject Tecumseh's
plan. As a compromise, Proctor suggested that they fall back
only as far as the Thames River and make a stand at Chatham
or Moraviantown.

Retreat

The retreat from Amherstburg included about eight hundred British regulars and a thousand warriors led by Tecumseh, accompanied by many women and children and a large amount of baggage.

As they left the smoking ruins of Fort Amherstburg behind, Tecumseh told his warriors, "We are now going to follow the British, and I feel certain that we shall never return." While Tecumseh's followers threatened to massacre the British if Proctor did not fight the Americans, many chiefs were hurrying to make peace with the advancing Americans.

On the evening of September 27, Proctor, Elliott and Tecumseh attended a banquet hosted by a fur trader and militia commander at Sandwich. Tecumseh ate with his pistols on either side of his plate and his hunting knife in front of it. The man who sat next to him said, "His bearing was irreproachable ... much better than that of some so-called gentlemen."

In the course of the evening, a messenger arrived with news that the American fleet had entered the Detroit River and was sailing north. Tecumseh picked up his pistols and told Proctor that they must go to meet the enemy and prevent him from going any farther. He reiterated how much better it would have been to stay at Amherstburg, where they could have taken their stand behind the great sandbanks of Elliott's point. "There, beyond any doubt, we could have kept the enemy from landing and have held our hunting grounds for our children."

Proctor disagreed with Tecumseh's suggestion and continued his retreat the next morning. Tecumseh and his warriors reluctantly followed, although Tecumseh stationed scouts along the riverbank to keep track of the American fleet and to fire on it occasionally. This gunfire convinced the commander of the American fleet to abandon his pursuit of the retreating forces and attach himself to Harrison's army. Tecumseh didn't destroy the bridges over which Harrison's army was pursuing them because he wanted to draw the Americans to Chatham, where Proctor had grudgingly promised to fight.

On October 3, Tecumseh and his warriors arrived at a gristmill owned by Benjamin Arnold, a militia captain whom Tecumseh had met at Fort Meigs. The British had set fire to a neighbouring mill a few days earlier. Tecumseh disapproved. Burning the gristmill seemed to him a wanton act of destruction with no military benefit and one that would cause much civilian hardship since people would no longer have a place to grind their grain. Tecumseh ordered that Arnold's mill not be destroyed. Arnold invited Tecumseh to dinner and to stay overnight. The next morning, Tecumseh remained at the mill until all the warriors had passed the area to ensure that his orders to spare the mill were followed. By this time, the pursuing Americans were nearing the mill. Despite the danger,

Tecumseh stopped long enough in his flight to drop off a bag of flour at the home of Arnold's brother-in-law, whose family had run out of food. Then a Native woman rowed Tecumseh across the river while his horse swam behind with Tecumseh holding its bridle.

Tecumseh decided Chatham would be a good place to make a stand against the Americans, since the community had a blockhouse. "Here," he told Lieutenant Colonel Augustus Warburton, Proctor's second-in-command, "we will either defeat Harrison or leave our bones."

Initially Warburton said that he would try to fulfill Proctor's pledge to make a stand at Chatham. However, the next morning he ordered his demoralized troops to withdraw towards Moraviantown. Having lost most of their baggage and food to the Americans, they were hungry and short of ammunition. Not only that, but the ground was soaked with recent rain.

Tecumseh decided to confront the Americans at Chatham without the support of the British. He stationed warriors at the bridges over the Thames River and McGregor's Creek, a sizable stream that merged with the Thames in Chatham. Harrison's forces arrived and attacked. Only two Americans were killed and six or seven wounded, while thirteen warriors were killed and many more wounded. Tecumseh was hit in the arm by a rifle ball, but he kept on fighting. Walk-in-the-Water and sixty of his Wyandot warriors defected to the Americans. Finally, Tecumseh decided they must abandon the fight and follow the British troops.

The Americans continued their pursuit. That night, Proctor and Tecumseh reconnoitred the American camp and considered attacking it but decided it was too strongly defended. On the morning of October 5, the American advance party captured more British boats laden with military stores and took another nine prisoners. As they proceeded, the Americans found a trail of abandoned stores.

Chapter Seven
The Battle of Moraviantown and After

Prepare a noble death song for the day when you go over the great divide.... When it comes your time to die... sing your death song and die like a hero going home. [Words attributed to Tecumseh]

Tecumseh spent the night before the Battle of Moraviantown (known to the Americans as the Battle of the Thames) with a small group of relatives and close friends, winding up his affairs. Earlier he had addressed his men. He predicted that he would not survive the coming battle and strongly suggested his men return home. "You needn't follow me, and there's every reason why you shouldn't follow me," he told them.

The Thames River was deep and ran between steep banks at the point where the battle took place. The banks were heavily treed, but with little underbrush. A short distance away a marsh ran nearly parallel to the river for about three kilometres. With the river guarding Proctor's left flank and the swamp his right flank, the battlefront was only about two hundred metres wide. Tecumseh placed half of his warriors on the far side of the swamp and took command there. The other half were under the command of Chippewa chief Oshawana (John Nahdee) in a larger swamp at right angles to Tecumseh.

By the time Tecumseh joined the British companies on the day of the battle he was so enraged by Proctor's continued reluctance to stand and fight that he threatened to shoot him. Colonel Elliott saved Proctor's life by throwing up the barrel of the gun that Tecumseh pointed at him. It was only then that Proctor reluctantly agreed to fight where they were.

The American forces, led by General Harrison, did not arrive until late afternoon. Tecumseh spent his time until then making a last-minute survey of the forces and offering encouragement. He even made peace of a sort with Proctor, advising him to "have a big heart. Tell your young men to be firm and all will be well." He walked along the main British line and shook each officer's hand. Then he returned to his warriors. "Be brave, stand firm, shoot straight," he told them.

Colonel Richard Johnson's "forlorn hope" Mounted Rifles squad from Kentucky led the attack against Tecumseh. "Forlorn hope" was a term referring to the first wave of soldiers in an attack. They were normally volunteers, and it was expected that most would be killed or injured.

Defiantly shouting "Remember River Raisin," Johnson's

Death of Tecumseh, by Nathaniel Currier, 1846

squad charged into the swamp. Initially the battle went well for Tecumseh. The "forlorn hope" had to dismount when their horses got bogged down on the swampy ground, and the warriors immediately engaged them in bitter hand-to-hand combat. When the warriors ran out of ammunition, they fought on with their hatchets. Soon all twenty of the cavalry squad lay dead or wounded.

A few minutes into the battle, Tecumseh approached Major Richardson's line. He pressed the hand of each officer as he passed and made appropriate remarks to each in Shawnee, which could be understood by the expressive signs accompanying them.

"Wherever the battle raged hottest, his own dauntless breast was seen in the van," wrote one early historian of Tecumseh. The warrior fell dead, however, not more than five minutes into the battle. His men continued to fight "with the frenzy of despair" until they learned that Proctor's line had broken and his men had abandoned them. Disheartened, the warriors "flung down their arms and fled."

An American cavalryman reported that he had heard Tecumseh trying to rally his men after the British line broke and Proctor ran off. "He yelled like a tiger, and urged his braves to the attack. We were then but a few yards apart."

Who Killed Tecumseh?

For many years debate raged over who killed Tecumseh and where he was buried. Neither question has ever been definitively answered. Some believed that he was killed by Colonel Johnson, leader of the "forlorn hope." They claimed that Tecumseh wounded Johnson and was about to kill him when Johnson shot him dead. American officials denied this story, and also denied charges that Tecumseh's body was mutilated — including one horrific story that his body was flayed and a razor strop made from his skin.

Ottawa and Chippewa warriors fighting alongside

Tecumseh just before his death said that Tecumseh's leg was broken by a musket ball and he told his warriors, "One of my legs is shot off. But leave me one or two guns loaded; I am going to have a last shot. Be quick and go!" These warriors admitted, however, that none of them actually saw Tecumseh die as American soldiers swarmed around him and they, the warriors, were forced away.

Black Hawk, a Sac war chief who claimed to have seen Tecumseh shot, did not accuse the Americans of mutilation. He said simply, "During the night we buried our dead, and brought off the body of Tecumseh, although we were in sight of the fires of the American camp." Legend has it that a select group of Shawnee warriors knew where Tecumseh was buried and that they have passed on this information from generation to generation up to the present day.

Another version of the story says that the man who carried Tecumseh's body from the battlefield was Chief Nahdee, Tecumseh's second-in-command at Moraviantown. In 1848, Chief Nahdee and his band moved to Walpole Island and brought Tecumseh's remains with them. Almost a century later, in 1931, Walpole Island's First World War veterans passed a resolution saying that Tecumseh's bones were there, and they raised a memorial cairn. The Island, now known as Walpole Island First Nation, is at the mouth of the St. Clair River on the Canadian side of the Ontario-Michigan border.

The following tribute to Tecumseh was written by an

unknown author:

Gloom, silence and solitude rest on the spot
Where the hopes of the red man perished.
But the fame of the hero who fell shall not
By the virtuous cease to be cherished.

Aftermath of Moraviantown

Proctor tried to defend himself against charges of incompetence following his retreat from Fort Amherstburg and the subsequent Battle of Moraviantown. In official letters he wrote that the Indians had executed their part "faithfully and courageously," and that if the troops had acted as he "confidently expected," he still believed they would have won the battle. He concluded, "With deep concern I mention the death of the chief Tecumseh."

Proctor did admit at least partial responsibility for the defeat, acknowledging that "sufficient attention had not been paid" to their boats during the retreat from Fort Amherstburg. As a result, boats, men, provisions, and all the un-issued ammunition had fallen into American hands.

After Tecumseh's death, some reports indicated that the British gave his son, Paukeesa (also known as Young Tecumseh), a commission in the British army, but this seems unlikely. Paukeesa was later appointed a village chief and received a stipend from the British until his death. The

Prophet spent the following winter trying to reassert his leadership and was chosen the principal chief of all the "Western Nations." When he was presented with a sword and pistols on behalf of the British monarchy, he promised "the most cordial cooperation" with the British forces and said that all the warriors down to "their smallest boys capable of bearing arms, shall be ready to march at a moment's notice."

Despite these words, The Prophet was reluctant to get involved in further conflict. He finally agreed to lead a war party to the Niagara frontier. The result was disastrous. He arrived after the battle had ended, and his sudden retreat the following day threatened the British position.

Following the defeat at Moraviantown, British officials repeatedly assured the Native people that they would never be abandoned and that England would soon send enough military reinforcements to defeat the Americans. Although the British had also promised on a number of occasions that they would not agree to peace without securing an autonomous First Nations territory, they did not keep their promise in the face of strong American opposition. The Treaty of Ghent, which ended the War of 1812, vaguely stated that Natives were given "all the rights and privileges they enjoyed before the war." The result of the treaty was a return to the status quo. On paper, it was almost as if the war had never been fought.

Most of the "American" warriors who had been allied

with the British signed a treaty in September 1815 that allowed them to return to their homes. The Prophet was not allowed to return until 1824 because he refused to sign the treaty.

Although neither the Americans nor the British can truly be said to have won the war, it was certainly lost by the Native people.

Epilogue

Little is known about Tecumseh's personal life, although he was apparently married four or five times between 1788 and 1795. He sent his first wife, who was Shawnee, back home to her parents for neglecting their baby. His sister Tecumapease likely raised that child, the son known as Paukeesa or Young Tecumseh. His second wife, Mamate, who was a mixed-blood Shawnee, died in childbirth. He had at least seven surviving children, and his three eldest sons fought with him at Moraviantown. Tecumseh's widow and some of their younger children remained with The Prophet for at least a short time after the war, as they relied on him for sustenance.

According to one story, Tecumseh told his brother-in-law the night before the Battle of Moraviantown that he did not want his eldest son to be elected as chief as he was "too much like a white man" because of his mother's mixed blood. This is unlikely. Tecumseh may have felt his eldest son would not make a good chief, but it could not have been due to his "white" blood since his mother was Shawnee.

Tecumseh in Legend and Mythology
Not surprisingly, in view of Tecumseh's fame and the lack of definite information about his personal life, many completely fictitious stories have grown up about him. The Prophet

started one of these stories long after Tecumseh's death, claiming that their father Puckshinwa's parents were a Creek warrior and the daughter of the governor of South Carolina, and that Puckshinwa was only later adopted by the Shawnee.

A second romantic legend involved Tecumseh and Rebecca Galloway, daughter of settlers in southern Ohio where Tecumseh was living in the years after Fallen Timbers. Galloway's great-grandson wrote a book claiming that Tecumseh had fallen in love with Rebecca. He said that the two had gone for canoe rides and that Rebecca had read some of Shakespeare's plays to Tecumseh. Tecumseh asked for her hand in marriage. Her family would only agree to the union if Tecumseh lived as a white man, and so no marriage took place.

A third story involves a family named Ice. The Ices claimed that Tecumseh's mother was a woman named Mary Bayles, who was stolen by the Shawnee as a young girl. Several years later, she returned home with a two-year-old son she called Tecumseh. She then married a man named Andrew Ice. Tecumseh lived with Mary and Andrew until he was 14 years old, when he returned to his father's people. Records indicate, however, that the Mary Bayles who married Andrew Ice was only about five years older than Tecumseh.

A fourth questionable story concerns Tecumseh's descendants and was reported in the 1880s. A Cherokee clergyman claimed that a Cherokee family named Proctor was descended from both Tecumseh and The Prophet. The fair-skinned branch of the family was descended from Tecumseh, while the darker Proctors were The Prophet's grandchildren.

One person who did have an authentic connection with Tecumseh was Stephen Ruddell, who was born in Kentucky the same year as Tecumseh (1768). In 1780 his family was captured during a battle between settlers and a group of Natives and Canadians. As a result, Stephen was adopted by a family living in the same village as Tecumseh and lived with the Shawnee for fifteen years. In 1840 he wrote a memoir of his time with Tecumseh. After the passage of so many years, Ruddell undoubtedly made some errors of fact and may also have exaggerated somewhat, but his admiration for Tecumseh is clear. He wrote that Tecumseh and he "became inseparable companions." Of Tecumseh's character he wrote, "There was a certain something in his countenance and manners that always commanded respect and at the same time made those about him love him."

Other information came from Ruddell's son, John, in letters written between 1863 and 1890. Some of that information was certainly incorrect or at least highly dubious. For instance, John says that Tecumseh received his mortal wound at the River Raisin Massacre rather than at the Battle of Moraviantown. In another place, he wrote, "My father was made a chief and was second in command to Tecumseh and had he remained with the Indians would in all probability have become his successor."

Although Stephen Ruddell made no comments about The Prophet in his manuscript, John wrote that his father thought Tecumseh would have been "a greater and better man" without the influence The Prophet had over him. John quoted his father as saying that it was the influence of The Prophet that caused Tecumseh to visit the Southern tribes to persuade them to "take up the hatchet against the Whites," and that he (Stephen) might have been able to prevent many Native warriors from fighting against the Americans in the War of 1812 if he could have spoken to Tecumseh before he went South. Stephen tried to convince Tecumseh that The Prophet possessed no supernatural powers and that revelations from the Great Spirit had closed. Tecumseh responded that such revelations might be closed to the white man but not to the Indian.

Tecumseh's Character and Legacy

Even many of his enemies believed that Tecumseh was both compassionate and a man of his word. Stories of his kindness abound, although many are likely apocryphal. One such story involved a clergyman captured at Detroit. Proctor proposed to imprison the clergyman because he wouldn't swear allegiance to the Crown. Tecumseh protested, and Proctor backed down when Tecumseh threatened to withdraw his support for the British.

Epilogue

In another story, Tecumseh saw a young American boy tending two oxen. Tecumseh's men needed food, so he took the oxen but promised to pay for them. When he asked the Indian Department to pay for the oxen, Elliott declared the oxen spoils of war and refused. Tecumseh insisted and even demanded an extra dollar for the boy's time and trouble in collecting payment.

Tecumseh gained the respect of a Canadian writer, John Charles Dent, in the 1880s because he "did us good service and died bravely fighting for our cause." However, Dent gently mocked "those enthusiastic hero-worshippers" who held Tecumseh up as a "warm and affectionate friend" of the British. "The simple truth is that Tecumseh would cheerfully have tomahawked every white man in American with his own hand had any opportunity of doing so been afforded him," Dent claimed.

Historian Henry Trumbull (1781–1843) considered Tecumseh "the most extraordinary Indian that has appeared in history" and said that even his harshest enemies credited him for his integrity and humanity.

American Brian Blodgett, a career army officer and a professor of military science, wrote in 1999 that Tecumseh wielded more power than any other North American Indian who ever lived, due to the strategic importance of his confederation, which had members from 32 different tribes (nations) spread across nearly 1.3 million square kilometres of territory. His death marked both the end of large-scale organized resistance to white settlement and of Native support for the British during the War of 1812. "When Tecumseh died, the British did not lose a subservient Indian leader, but a man more powerful and capable than any British officer in the western theatre," according to Blodgett.

Another modern American professor of military history, Don Hickey, offers a minority view. He says that one of the leading myths about the War of 1812 has to do with the importance of Tecumseh in fighting that war. Hickey admits that Tecumseh was undeniably the pre-eminent Indian war chief in the Northwest, but he says that the Northwest was the least important theatre of operations during the war. He also charges that Tecumseh played a role in the defeat at Moraviantown when he insisted on making "an ill-advised stand" there. Finally, Hickey says that Tecumseh did not eclipse The Prophet in importance until after the defeat at Tippecanoe and thus was important for only a very short time.

A second myth, according to Hickey, was that members of the militia were of crucial importance during the war. In fact, Hickey says, the real work was done "by British regulars with an important assist from their native allies."

Canadian historian Ron Dale says that The Prophet should be given more credit — and Tecumseh less — for their activities both before and during the War of 1812. Dale suggests that Harrison deliberately built up Tecumseh to become more important than other Native leaders in order to cause jealousy and thus reduce Tecumseh's prestige among his people during the War. Dale also believes that both Stephen Ruddell's reminiscences of Tecumseh, and those of Benjamin Drake in a biography of Tecumseh and The Prophet, "surfaced as part of the campaign" to elect William Henry Harrison as president of the United States in 1840. Harrison's "whole campaign was based on his military deeds in defeating Tecumseh." The idea was to build Tecumseh up as "a larger than life military strategist of awesome abilities. At the same time, The Prophet was belittled and besmirched."

Evidence of Tecumseh's enduring legacy abounds. Naturally there are many Internet websites about Tecumseh the man. In addition, at least seven cities and towns and two mountains bear his name — to say nothing of innumerable schools and other institutions and businesses. The Tecumseh Power Company, which has been manufacturing small engines since 1895, is possibly the best-known business. Then there was General William Tecumseh Sherman (1820–91), one of the leading generals on the Union side during the American Civil War. He wrote in his memoirs that his family and friends always called him "Cump."

At least two cities regularly pay tribute to Tecumseh. Chillicothe, Ohio, has staged an annual outdoor drama about the great warrior since the 1970s. And Chatham, Ontario, commemorates life circa 1812 during Upper Canada Heritage Days. This celebration includes historical recreations of War of 1812 battles. Actors portraying Tecumseh and other notable characters also recount events leading up to the war.

List of Historical Figures

Arnold, Benjamin. Former American militia captain, who later became a mill owner in Upper Canada.

Big Warrior. Creek chief whom Tecumseh met on his southern tour.

Black Hawk. Sac (Sauk) war chief who was with Tecumseh at the Battle of Moraviantown.

Black Hoof (Catahecassa). Shawnee chief who signed the Treaty of Greenville and kept most Shawnee from supporting Tecumseh.

Blackfish. Shawnee chief at Chillicothe when Tecumseh was a child. He may have been the adoptive father of Stephen Ruddell.

Blue Jacket. Shawnee war chief, leader at Battle of Fallen Timbers. (See also Little Turtle).

Brock, Sir Isaac. Commander-in-chief of the troops

in Upper Canada until his death at the Battle of Queenston Heights.

Brush, Captain Henry. American who was in charge of a supply train sent to Detroit early in the War of 1812.

Campbell, Major William. Commander of British Fort Miami at the time of the Battle of Fallen Timbers.

Changing Feathers (Penagashea). Prominent Shawnee medicine man, who became a mentor to Lalawethika (later known as The Prophet)

Cheesuaka (Cheeseekau or Chiksika). Older brother of Tecumseh, who was killed at the Battle of Buchanan's Station in 1792.

Claus, William. Deputy Superintendent of the British Indian Department, circa 1807.

Cornstalk. Shawnee chief who represented his people at the first two Indian treaties negotiated with the Americans at the time of the American Revolution.

Craig, Sir James Henry. Governor-in-chief of Upper Canada, circa 1805, and Governor General of Canada, 1807–11.

List of Historical Figures

Dale, Sam. American general who witnessed Tecumseh's meeting with the Creek.

Dudley, Colonel William. American commander killed at the Siege of Fort Meigs.

Elliott, Matthew. Superintendent of British Indian Department at Fort Amherstburg in 1808, who fought as a colonel in the War of 1812.

Harrison, William Henry. Governor of Indiana Territory, military leader during the War of 1812 and briefly president of the United States.

Heald, Captain Nathan. Commander at Fort Dearborn at the time of the massacre in 1812.

Hoentubbee. Choctaw chief whom Tecumseh met on his southern tour.

Hull, William. American brigadier general who surrendered Detroit.

Johnson, Colonel Richard. Commander who fought against Tecumseh at the Battle of Moraviantown and later (1837–1841) became vice-president of the United States.

Kenton, Simon. A Kentucky frontiersman with whom Tecumseh had several run-ins.

Lalawethika. Younger brother of Tecumseh (see The Prophet).

Leatherlips. Wyandot chief and rival of Tecumseh, put to death for witchcraft.

Little Turtle. Miami chief who, along with Blue Jacket and Roundhead, was a leader of the confederacy that opposed the Americans during the Northwest Indian War.

Main Poche (Withered or Black Hand). A Potawatomi chief at the time of the Battle of Tippecanoe.

Methotaske (Methoataaskee). Mother of Tecumseh.

Muir, Captain Adam. British Commander at the Siege of Fort Meigs.

Nahdee, John (Oshawana). Tecumseh's second-in-command at Moraviantown.

Pokagon, Leopold and Simon. Father and son, both Potawatomi chiefs.

Pontiac. Ottawa chief who led a struggle against the British in the 1760s.

Proctor, Henry (sometimes spelled Procter). A British commander during War of 1812.

Prevost, George. Governor General of Upper Canada during the War of 1812.

Puckshinwah (sometimes Pukeshinwah, Pukeshinewa or Pucksinwa). Shawnee chief and father of Tecumseh.

Pushmataha. A Choctaw chief who opposed Tecumseh's confederacy plan.

Richardson, Major John. Fought alongside Tecumseh (whom he had known since childhood) at the siege of Fort Meigs and the Battle of Moraviantown.

Roundhead. Wyandot chief who led warriors at the battle of Raisin River and the siege of Fort Meigs. (See also Little Turtle).

Ruddell, Stephen. American who spent fiftern years living with the Shawnee after being captured as a boy.

Stone Eater. Wea war chief and a leader at the Battle of Tippecanoe.

Tecumapease. Sister of Tecumseh.

The Prophet (Tenskwatawa). Younger brother of Tecumseh, originally called Lalawethika.

Walk-in-the-Water. Wyandot leader who fought at Raisin River and defected to the Americans before the Battle of Moraviantown.

Warburton, Lieutenant Colonel Augustus. Proctor's second-in-command at the Battle of Moraviantown.

Wayne, General Anthony. American commander at the Battle of Fallen Timbers.

Weld, Isaac. Described gift-giving by the British Indian Department at Fort Amherstburg.

White Loon. Shawnee leader at the Battle of Tippecanoe.

Winnemac. Potawatomi leader at the Battle of Tippecanoe.

Bibliography

The following are a few of the most important sources used in researching this book. The older books are all available online.

Beard, Reed. *The Battle of Tippecanoe*. 4th ed. Chicago: Hammond Press, 1911. (1st ed., 1889.)

Brice, Wallace A. *History of Fort Wayne*. Fort Wayne, Indiana: D.W. Jones & Son, 1868.

Dillon, John B. *History of Indiana*. Indianapolis: Bingham & Doughty, 1859.

Dowd, Gregory Evans. *A Spirited Resistance: The North American Indian Struggle for Unity, 1745–1815*. Baltimore: Johns Hopkins University Press, 1992.

Drake, Benjamin. *Life of Tecumseh and of His Brother the Prophet*. Cincinnati: E. Morgan & Company, 1841.

Hitsman, J. Mackay. *The Incredible War of 1812: A Military History*. Revised by Donald E. Graves. Toronto: Robin Brass Studio, 1999.

Klinck, Carl F. (ed.) *Tecumseh: Fact and Fiction in Early Records*. Ottawa: Tecumseh Press, 1978.

Lomax, D. A. N. *A history of the Services of the 41st (the Welch) Regiment*. Devonport: Caxton Press, 1899.

Lossing, Benson J. *The Pictorial Field-Book of the War of 1812*. New York: Harper & Brothers, 1868.

Strefoff, Rebecca. *Tecumseh and the Shawnee Confederation*. New York: Facts-on-File, 1998.

Tunnell, Major Harry D. IV. *To Compel with Armed Force: A Staff Ride Handbook for the Battle of Tippecanoe*. Fort Leavenworth, Kansas: Combat Studies Institute, n. d.

Tupper, Ferdinand Brock. *The Life and Correspondence of Sir Isaac Brock*. London: Simpkin, Marshall, & Co., 1845.

Turner, Wesley. *The War of 1812: The War that Both Sides Won*. Toronto: Dundurn Press, 1990.

Wood, William. *Select British Documents of the Canadian War of 1812*. 3 vols. Toronto: Champlain Society, 1920–28.

Information about Simon Kenton comes from the following articles, available online:

Backs, Jean. "Simon Kenton, Frontier Hero." *Ohio State Parks Magazine*, Fall 2003/ Winter 2004.

McFarland, R.W. "Simon Kenton," *Ohio History*, 13, no. 1 (Jan. 1904).

The Galafilm War of 1812 website is at www.galafilm.com/1812/e/index.html

Photo Credits

About the Author

Irene Ternier Gordon, who lives along the historic Assiniboine River just west of Winnipeg, grew up on a grain farm in west-central Saskatchewan. She has had a passion for history, reading and writing since childhood. After a career as a teacher-librarian, she became a freelance writer in 1998. This is her sixth book.

Irene and her husband, Don, enjoy travelling, canoeing, hiking, skiing, and sailing. Above all, she likes to spend time with her three young grandsons: Jesse, Riley, and Felix.

Index

Index